Murdered with Straight Lines

Drawings of Bristol by *Garth England*

Edited by Jes Fernie and Theresa Bergne

Contents

Come and See, Alan
Introductory essay by Jes Fernie

Notes on *Future Perfect*

Garth England delivering milk, January 1963.
Taken outside 68 Melbury Road, Knowle.

Come and See, Alan

Garth England was born in Bristol General Hospital in 1935, four years before World War II broke out. His mother named him after a blind pianist in a romantic novel by Florence Barclay, a blockbuster in its day. With the exception of a brief period in Germany in the 1950s when he did National Service, Garth spent all of his seventy-nine years living in neighbourhoods in south Bristol: Knowle West, Hengrove, Totterdown and Bedminster.

Throughout his life Garth held a series of jobs that embedded him within the community in which he lived and worked. As a paperboy, telegram boy, milkman and railway man, he was a regular fixture on the local landscape; a friendly presence who understood the rhythm of the neighbourhood, as well as its unique social and architectural character.

At the age of seventy, when he moved into a residential care home, Garth began to map out the details of his life. Using A4 sheets of paper, coloured pencils and his formidable memory, he recorded, in painstaking detail, the buildings, people, conversations and stories that he had amassed over time. Most of the works, completed between 2006 and 2013, were drawn from memory, some from photographs, while others were 'purely imaginary'.

In 2013, Jo Plimmer, an engagement manager working on a contemporary art project called Future Perfect, visited Hengrove Lodge to talk to Garth about the history of the area, with the aim of incorporating photographs and drawings into a curtain in Hengrove Community Centre. After talking together for a while, Garth very modestly suggested that Jo 'might be interested' in looking at some of his drawings that he kept on a shelf in his room.

This book is made up of a selection of these remarkable drawings. Together they tell the poignant story of a childhood lived through a world war and its aftermath; the development of Britain's Welfare State and social housing provision; vernacular architecture and the rise of modernism. Garth charts the introduction of fitted kitchens and flushable toilets. He sets out beautifully the change of fashion in furniture from heavy, wooden dressers owned by grand-parents across the land in the 1950s, to the more contemporary designs bought by his parents, with jaunty angled legs and melamine surfaces. Strides in public health and welfare were also being made, as is evident in Garth's note that in 1950 cardboard tops on milk bottles were replaced with tin foil, and it became illegal to sell milk straight from the churn. There is a clear sense that life is better, cleaner and brighter in this new post-war world.

All these societal changes provide the backdrop to a series of personal stories that create a rich, often humorous narrative. A telephone wire suspended between a childhood home and a garden shed is used by Garth and his brothers to call their dad to tea; neighbours engage in a twenty year dispute over the design of a garage roof; Garth gives his mother a lampshade won in a raffle for her birthday and makes a daisy chain for a girl called Violet; he fashions plant pots out of old '78 records; and in 1956 he buys his first car for £30 (a 1935 Austin 7 Ruby Saloon). There is even mention of a notorious unsolved murder at the Lloyds Bank in Knowle West in 1949.

Teachers are defined by the architecture of their houses. Mr Burt, the headmaster, owns a house with green and yellow window frames, while the house belonging to Miss Gay, a primary school teacher, is slightly less grand, with its side entrance and absent garage. Garth's piano teacher's home receives special treatment, with a detailed drawing of a handsome bay-fronted stone house, a well-kept garden, a garage and steps leading up to the front door. Garth is careful to tell us the names of the sisters who run the music school and goes on to note that he 'was a disaster' at piano.

His job as a milkman dictates the terms of his relationship with the architecture around him. While most people walk up the steps of a house and enter through the front door as the inhabitant or a visitor, a delivery person only experiences the façade, surrounding landscape and, occasionally, the owner. Next to some of his drawings, Garth makes notes about the unique characteristics of either the architecture, the owners, or the vicious dogs in the houses to which he delivers milk: 'House of Many Steps', 'Beware of the Dog' and 'Bible punching Bessie'. In some cases, it seems like the houses are speaking directly to us, assuming the guise of the owner: 'Round the Back if you don't mind' and 'Don't bring your float here!'

Garth clearly felt a sense of pride about his home and neighbourhood throughout his life. When he is evacuated to Glastonbury during the war, he makes friends with a little boy called Alan. Garth decides, age six, that he wants to show Alan where he lives and the pair of them set off on the twenty-three mile journey on foot to Bristol ('Come and see, Alan'). Needless to say, they don't get very far.

While most of the drawings are jovial and good-humoured, there are some that strike a more sombre tone. He is clearly disturbed by his experience of being evacuated; in one drawing he is confused and hurt when he is given a sandwich and told to sit separately at supper while the family enjoys a cooked meal at the table. Later, in the same sequence, a child is seen holding on to an adult's hand with the words 'please take me home' written below. When he is stationed in Germany in the mid-1950s, he witnesses a soldier's request for compassionate leave being turned down. Garth says 'they treated him like he was a criminal'. Towards the end of his working life, one of Garth's colleagues is killed while cycling to work to do Garth's nightshift. In relaying these incidents, Garth's matter of fact delivery emphasises the beguiling, unsentimental nature of his project, and his approach to life in general.

Many readers who know Bristol well will recognise some of the buildings and companies that are depicted in the book: Bristol Royal Infirmary, St Werburgh's Church, Temple Meads train station, and Bristol New Gaol (where the last execution took place in Britain in 1964) are all here. As are A.E. Tozer & Family, proprietors of the Jubilee Road Dairy that Garth worked for (immortalised by Tozers Hill in current day Knowle); Udall's bike shop; and Jones the butchers on St John's Lane in Bedminster.

Garth never claimed to be an architectural historian or social commentator. He was the first to acknowledge that some of the architectural details in his drawings were inaccurate. What he is doing here isn't necessarily about attempting to capture reality; it seems more to be about conveying a sense of the past in order to reflect on the present and consider a life well lived.

This book is being published at a particular moment in British history when the Welfare State is slowly being dismantled and community life is unraveling. Garth's drawings are a testament to the achievements of twentieth-century Britain and a call to arms for an ongoing commitment to the greater good. In a sense, we, the readers, have taken the place of Alan, Garth's childhood friend. We are being shown what it means to live in a community, to notice the small things, and celebrate the creative potential of every individual.

Garth died in 2014, but he knew of our plans to publish his drawings and gave us his blessing. When we asked him what he'd like the book to be called, he said 'Murdered with straight lines – that's what my art teacher used to say about my drawings. He didn't like the way I always used a ruler'.

Jes Fernie
Independent curator and co-curator of *Future Perfect*, 2016

Childhood 1935 – 1945

I FIRST SAW THE LIGHT OF DAY
FROM THIS HOSPITAL ON THE
27TH OF APRIL 1935 THE SECOND
SON OF A SECOND SON I WAS JUST
IN TIME FOR KING GEORGE V SILVER
JUBILEE CELEBRATIONS ON 6TH MAY.
THE GROUNDFLOOR WAS USED AS
WAREHOUSES ORIGINALY.

THE BATHURST TAVERN.

FROM A PAINTING
BY SAMUEL JACKSON
1794-1869, (WITHOUT
ITS BALCONY) BUT WITH
AN EXTRA LINE OF THE
WINDOWS.

E C England 2007

WHEN MY PARENTS WERE MARRIED IN 1932 THEY WENT TO LIVE AT 5 MARLING RD NEARBY. HERE MUM RAN A SMALL LOCAL SHOP WHILE DAD WAS A BUILDERS LABOURER. AT A LATER STAGE THEY BOUGHT 30 GLENBURN RD FOR A DEPOSIT OF £20. AT THAT TIME A £1 WEEKLY WOULD COVER THEIR OUTGOINGS. I WAS THEIR SECOND SON AS MARGARET JOY NEVER ARRIVED (A DAUGHTER) WAITING FOR MY ARRIVAL AT BGH MUM WAS READING AN EDWARDIAN NOVEL CALLED "THE ROSARY" BY FLORENCE BARCLAY. IT FEATURED A BLIND PIANIST DR GARTH. IT WAS A STORY WITH A LADY LOVE. THIS I BELIEVE WAS THE FIRST MALE CHRISTIAN NAME TO HAND. ON MY ARRIVAL. AS I WAS SO YOUNG THEN THE DRAWING ABOVE IS ONLY IN MY IMAGINATION.

G A England 2013.

A view of Dads Greenhouse etc.
The wire was our phone link to
tell him tea was ready. In his

Oposite
Garden
Shed
Green
House And
Coldframe

Chicken
Coop

Bonfire
And Comp
Ost

Shed he would spend hours making the most beautiful fishing
rods. Eventualy they became lon
-ger than the shed itself hence
the hole at side of the door. He
would leave it locked while
at work. However we boys wou
-ld simply put a hand inside
the hole and release the
catch. Usefull when you need
-ed to borrow his tools. We
had moved here from rooms
at 3 Holmesdale Rd Victoria
Park. The rear of which
could be seen from 288 Red
-catch Rd, my adult home
for 35 years. Paultow Ave also
was just around the corner
from Holmesdale Rd. At Spring
leaze old Mr Manning would
repare our shoes and Mr Nurcombe
was the manager of a local
co-op store. Mother was born
Rosina Hester Thomas at Holmes
Hill Rd on 4th March 1911. After
3 marriages she died at Maesknol on the
28th Oct 1997 (England, Hayman, Brackley)
and her ashes scattered in the Bristol
channel at Portishead. Her wish.!

Mr Tanner 84 Broadfield Rd

Downstairs.

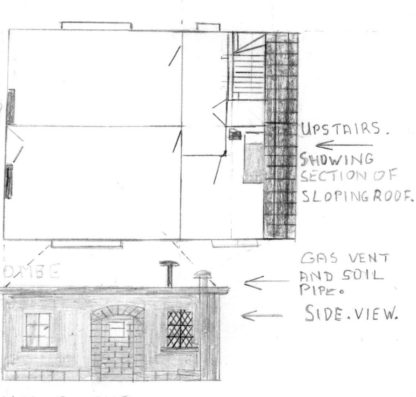

Upstairs.
Showing
section of
sloping roof.

Gas vent
and soil
pipe.
Side. View.

Within These Walls.

G A England 2010

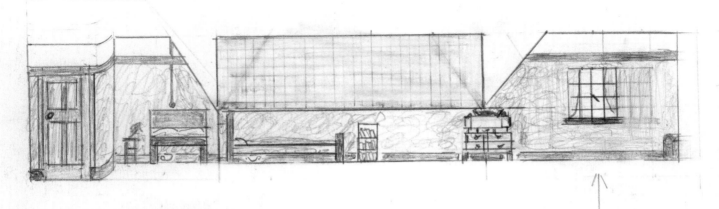

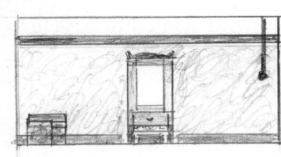

From the window could
be seen the top of the
speedway/greyhound
scoreboard. On Friday
evenings it was a constant
BRRM BRRM BRRM.

14 Paultow Ave.

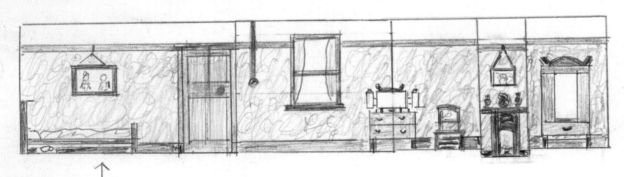

My Mothers Fathers

Parents.

My Parents Home At Top   Built 1931/2. If the Area Between Us

Had Not Been Developt, Later I Would Very Likely Had Been Able To See Hengrove

Lodge In The Distance. Grandma Was A Victorian Lady Hence Profuse With Pictur-

-es And Ornaments. Over The Bed "The Lord Shall Be Thy Confidence." Is Stated.

                    G.A England 2006.

A PRESENT FOR MY
PARENTS ON THEIR
SILVER WEDDING 1957.

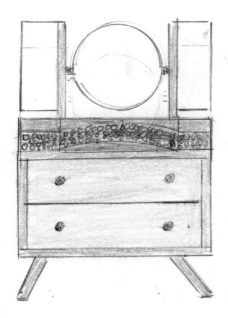

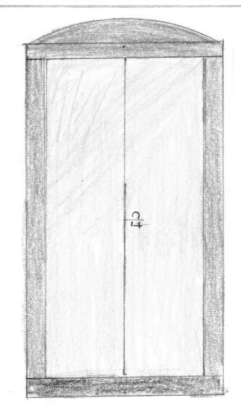

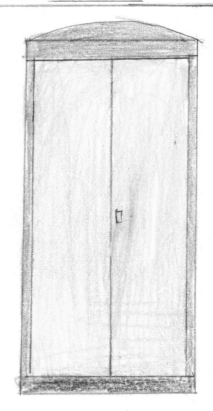

A BACHELOR
BEDROOM SUITE.
AT 86 REDCATCH Rd.

DADS WRIT
ING DESK
AND SMOKIN
G CABINET

MY BOOKCASE
(HOMEMADE).

HOURS OF ENJOYMENT
WITH MY BOOKS AND
GRAMOPHONE RECORDS
78 R.P.M. OLD ONES
MADE USEFULL BULB
HOLDERS.

G A England 2012.

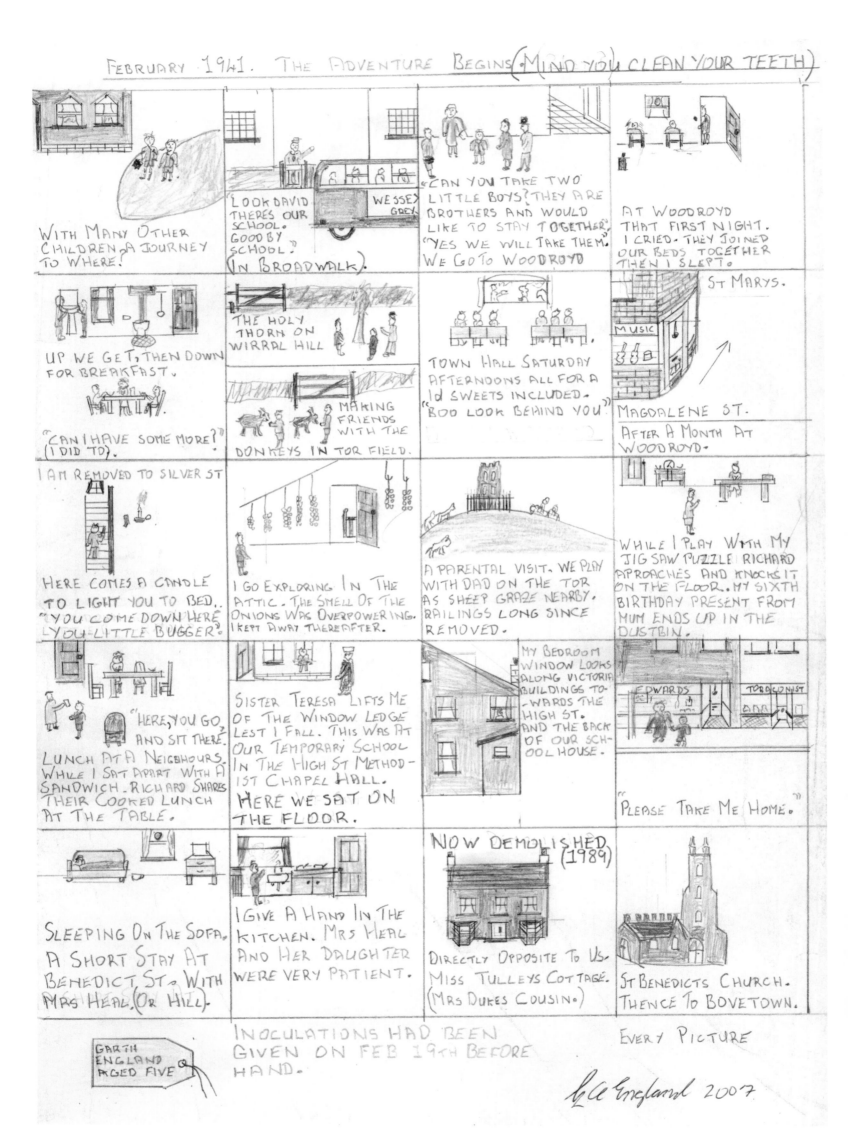

WITH MANY OTHER CHILDREN A JOURNEY TO WHERE!

LOOK DAVID THERES OUR SCHOOL. GOOD BY SCHOOL." (IN BROADWALK).

WESSEX GREY

"CAN YOU TAKE TWO LITTLE BOYS? THEY ARE BROTHERS AND WOULD LIKE TO STAY TOGETHER." "YES WE WILL TAKE THEM." WE GO TO WOODROYD

AT WOODROYD THAT FIRST NIGHT. I CRIED. THEY JOINED OUR BEDS TOGETHER THEN I SLEPT.

UP WE GET, THEN DOWN FOR BREAKFAST.
"CAN I HAVE SOME MORE?" (I DID TO).

THE HOLY THORN ON WIRRAL HILL

MAKING FRIENDS WITH THE DONKEYS IN TOR FIELD.

TOWN HALL SATURDAY AFTERNOONS ALL FOR A 1d SWEETS INCLUDED. "BOO LOOK BEHIND YOU."

ST MARYS.
MUSIC
MAGDALENE ST.
AFTER A MONTH AT WOODROYD.

I AM REMOVED TO SILVER ST
HERE COMES A CANDLE TO LIGHT YOU TO BED. "YOU COME DOWN HERE YOU LITTLE BUGGER".

I GO EXPLORING IN THE ATTIC. THE SMELL OF THE ONIONS WAS OVERPOWERING. I KEPT AWAY THEREAFTER.

A PARENTAL VISIT. WE PLAY WITH DAD ON THE TOR AS SHEEP GRAZE NEARBY. RAILINGS LONG SINCE REMOVED.

WHILE I PLAY WITH MY JIG SAW PUZZLE RICHARD APPROACHES AND KNOCKS IT ON THE FLOOR. MY SIXTH BIRTHDAY PRESENT FROM MUM ENDS UP IN THE DUSTBIN.

"HERE, YOU GO, AND SIT THERE."
LUNCH AT A NEIGHBOURS. WHILE I SAT APART WITH A SANDWICH. RICHARD SHARES THEIR COOKED LUNCH AT THE TABLE.

SISTER TERESA LIFTS ME OF THE WINDOW LEDGE LEST I FALL. THIS WAS AT OUR TEMPORARY SCHOOL IN THE HIGH ST METHODIST CHAPEL HALL. HERE WE SAT ON THE FLOOR.

MY BEDROOM WINDOW LOOKS ALONG VICTORIA BUILDINGS TOWARDS THE HIGH ST. AND THE BACK OF OUR SCHOOL HOUSE.

EDWARDS
TOBACCONIST
"PLEASE TAKE ME HOME."

SLEEPING ON THE SOFA. A SHORT STAY AT BENEDICT ST. WITH MRS HEAL (OR HILL).

I GIVE A HAND IN THE KITCHEN. MRS HEAL AND HER DAUGHTER WERE VERY PATIENT.

NOW DEMOLISHED (1989)
DIRECTLY OPPOSITE TO US. MISS TULLEYS COTTAGE. (MRS DUKES COUSIN.)

ST BENEDICTS CHURCH. THENCE TO BOVETOWN.

GARTH ENGLAND AGED FIVE

INOCULATIONS HAD BEEN GIVEN ON FEB 19th BEFORE HAND.

EVERY PICTURE

L A England 2007

I AWAIT MY FATE. SO I

DECIDE TO RE ARRANGE THE PARLOUR. "WHAT ARE YOU DOING MY LOVE? SHE SAID ON FINDING ME IN ACTION. (NELLIE).

POUNDS SHILLINGS AND PENCE THE COW JUMPED OVER THE FENCE, SHE CAUGHT HER TAIL ON A RUSTY NAIL, POUNDS SHILLINGS AND PENCE. A FOURTEEN YEAR OLD GIRL READS TO ME. I HAVE NOT SEEN HER SINCE, SHE WOULD NOW BE NEAR EIGHTY YEARS OF AGE SURNAME PETERS.

PRAISE BE

THE GREEDY FOWLS PECK AT OUR FALLEN TEA TIME CRUMBS. THEY WERE BRO -UGH HOME BECAUSE THEY WERE NOT WELL.

← THERE GARTH DID YOU LIKE THAT I WAS ASKED?

WC

THE KITCHEN AT BOVETOWN.

UP OVER WOODEN HILL

WE HELP IN THE FIELD.

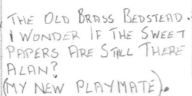

SHE LOVES ME SHE LOVES ME NOT

MAKING DAISY CHAINS FOR VIOLET. HER BIG SISTER READ TO ME.

FAIRYLAND TO ME.

ACTUALY WICK HOLLOW.

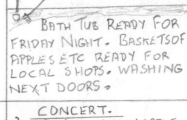

BATH NIGHT AT BOVETOWN.

VIOLET AND I PART.

THE LITTLE TIN BRIDGE. WITH A NEW PLAYMATE.

GLASTONBURY 2M →
← BRISTOL 23M
COME AND SEE ALAN.

THE OLD BRASS BEDSTEAD. I WONDER IF THE SWEET PAPERS ARE STILL THERE ALAN? (MY NEW PLAYMATE).

I COLLECT FIREWOOD.

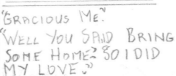

"GRACIOUS ME." "WELL YOU SAID BRING SOME HOME? SO I DID MY LOVE."

OUT THE BACK.

BATH TUB READY FOR FRIDAY NIGHT. BASKETS OF APPLES ETC READY FOR LOCAL SHOPS. WASHING NEXT DOORS.

BOTTOM OF BOVETOWN. THIMBLE COTTAGE.

TOWARDS THE TOP.

STONE BULWARKS.

SUNDAY EVENING CHAPEL.

OH PRESTBON SINNER MAY I COME IN? ♪♫♯♫♯♫ (FROM AN UNKNOWN HYMN)

TEMPERANCE MEETING

EXIT

THE DEMON DRINK DEMO -NSTRATION WITH A DEAD FLY A GLASS OF WATER AND ONE OF ALCOHOL. (THE FLY DIED HAPPY).

CONCERT.

I'L BE WITH YOU IN APPLE BLOSSOM TIME, I'L BE WITH YOU TO HOLD YOUR HAND IN MINE, ONE DAY IN MAY WE'L NAME THE DAY, HAPPY WE'L BE ON THIS OUR WEDDING-DAY. ♪♫♯♫♯♫ (ALL WITHOUT AMPLIFIER).

BUSHEY COOMBE.

VIEWED FROM THE FIELD.

HIGH ST CHAPEL.

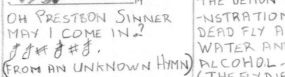

TEMP'Y SCHOOL HERE.

ALL MY OWN WORK.

TEA POT STAND AND KETTLE HOLDER WOVEN WITH ORANGE AND GREEN WOOL ON CARDBOARD BASE FOR BACK HOME.

BUS STOP   BRISTO

ITS BEEN A LONG 16 MONTHS I CAME HERE A CRY BABY. NOW A BIG BOY MY TIME AWAY HAS TAUGHT ME A LOT ABOUT LIFE AND ITS PROBLEMS. I WAS NOW SEVEN YEARS OLD - ITS JULY 1942.

TELLS A STORY.

KINDLY COUNTRY PEOPLE FILLED WITH LOVE GALORE.

E C England 2004

Both 13 Silver St and 24 Bovetown had no electricity or bathroom. Even the gas supply was downstairs

St Peters Church Draycott Som.

From a Photo. Mr Mrs Anderson. †

only. Both had a galvanized bath tub for Friday nights in front of the fire or in the kitchen. A hot water supply would be obtained from the kitchen clothes boiler. Silver streets toilet was outside but Bovetowns had been built at some time in the kitchen area, out of the question now. At Bovetown the tub would be kept outside hung on the wall by a rusty nail. Silver street had a gas stove but Bovetown only a kitchen range, this would be kept going daily throughout the year for cooking purposes. Two Sound flat irons would have to be hot. When one cooled down you would simply change them over. A jug and basin would be in your bedroom, sometimes with a matching chamber pot for your ablutions. Hot water if you were lucky. If not tough luck. Bovetown would originaly had an outside privvy, there was no flush sanitation in 1959. Water would be obtained from the nearest well or a drayman would call and sell you some.

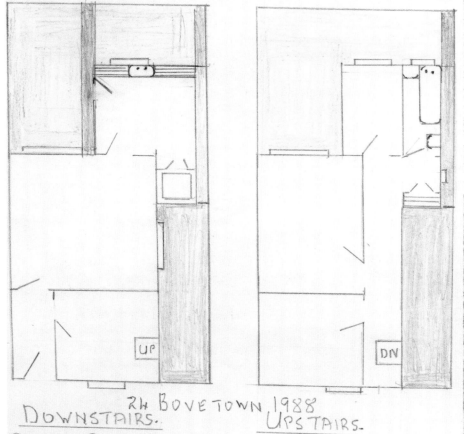

Downstairs.

24 Bovetown 1988
Upstairs.

Area Exterior. Shaded.

G A England

UP

DN

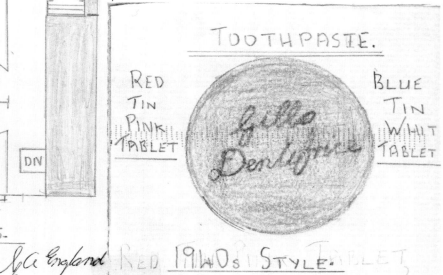

Toothpaste.

Red Tin Pink Tablet

Gibbs Dentifrice

Blue Tin Whit Tablet

Red 1940s Style. Tablet

PLAN OF 2h BOVETOWN 1941 CIRCA 1759.   FRONTAGE.

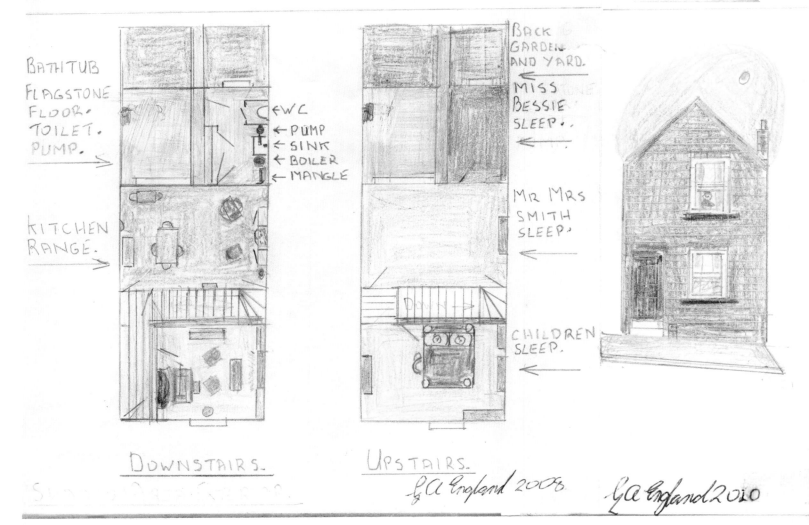

BATHTUB
FLAGSTONE
FLOOR.
TOILET.
PUMP.

KITCHEN
RANGE.

← WC
← PUMP
← SINK
← BOILER
← MANGLE

BACK
GARDEN
AND YARD.

MISS
BESSIE
SLEEP.

Mr Mrs
SMITH
SLEEP.

CHILDREN
SLEEP.

DOWNSTAIRS.   UPSTAIRS.
G A England 2008.   G A England 2010

THE LIVING ROOM AT 2h BOVETOWN 1941.   CIRCA 1759.

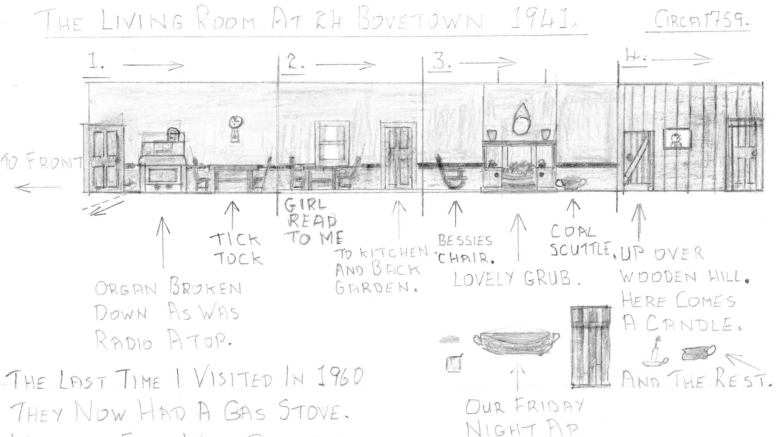

1. →   2. →   3. →   4. →

TO FRONT

TICK
TOCK

GIRL
READ
TO ME

TO KITCHEN
AND BACK
GARDEN.

BESSIES
CHAIR.
LOVELY GRUB.

COAL
SCUTTLE.

UP OVER
WOODEN HILL.
HERE COMES
A CANDLE.
AND THE REST.

ORGAN BROKEN
DOWN AS WAS
RADIO ATOP.

THE LAST TIME I VISITED IN 1960
THEY NOW HAD A GAS STOVE.
NOUGHT ELSE WAS CHANGED
AND I FANCY NEVER WAS.
HOME TO GEORGE NELLIE AND BESSIE.

OUR FRIDAY
NIGHT AP
-OINTMENT.
IN FRONT OF
THE FIRE.
G A England 2009

BOTH FROM PHOTO'S.
EXCEPT THE CAR.

THAT PINT
OF MILK HAS
ARRIVED SIR.
TUZERS RED
TOP FROM
BRISTOL.
DEMOLISHED
1990. SADLY.

GLOVEMAKING
WORKSHOP.
←

HUGH MONTESORI -
PRIVATE SCHOOL
NEXT DOOR. HERE

CIRCA 1860.

GLASTONBURY
POLICE
STATION.

NOW
APPARTMENTS.

AT MISS TULLEYS COTTAGE I HAD
MY LAST MEETING WITH MR DUKE DEC 1988.
(FORMERLY OF WOODROYD, STREET RD 1941).

IT WAS UNFORTUNATELY
SADLY DEMOLISHED 1989.
FOR A SLIP RD.

G A England
2007

A.38.

VILLAGE. →

← WINFORD HOSPITAL.

ON RETURNING TO SPRINGLEAZE IN EARLY 1941 THE HOUSE HAD BEEN DAMAGED PROBABLY IN THE RAID OF NOV 25TH 1940. CEILINGS WERE DOWN AND DOORS BLOWN OF. BY THE TIME OF THE NEXT RAID AT EASTER 1941 DAVID AND I HAD BEEN EVACUATED TO GLASTONBURY. AT CHRISTMAS 1940 WE HAD VERY HEAVY SNOW. MUMS MUSTARD COLOURED JUMPER WAS FROZEN SOLID ON THE CLOTHES LINE. ONE DAY A POLICEMAN CALLED ON MY BEHALF AS I HAD BEEN OBSERVED TOUCHING THE LOCAL COUNTRY BUS AS IT WOUND ITS WAY UP THE HILL TOWARDS THE A38 AND BRISTOL. I ALSO TOUCHED THE COMBUSTION STOVE WITH MY RIGHT HAND. THE SCAR REMAINS. BOTH INCIDENTS THROUGH A DARE. THE INNOCENSE OF CHILDHOOD!.

TWO NIGHTS AT IRON ACTON.

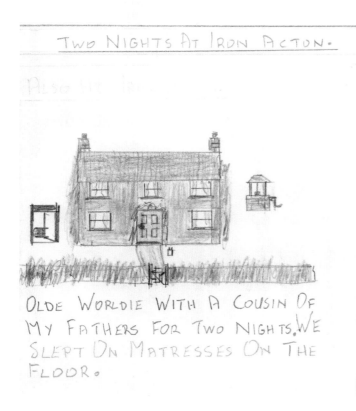

OLDE WORLDIE WITH A COUSIN OF MY FATHERS FOR TWO NIGHTS. WE SLEPT ON MATRESSES ON THE FLOOR.

BACK IN BRISTOL

THE HOME IN MERFIELD RD OF MY FIRST SCHOOL TEACHER MISS MARY MERCHANT. AT KNOWLE PARK INFANTS 1940.

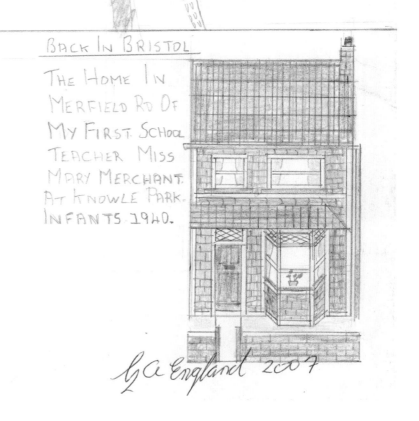

G C England 2007

SOME OF GRANDMAS FURNITURE I REMEMBER

MY BEDROOM WHEN I
STAYED AT IN PAULTOW
AVE WINDMILL HILL.

BIBLE TEXT

The Lord
Shall Be
thy
Confidence

DOWNSTAIRS.

CHEFANEIR
(SIDEBOARD)

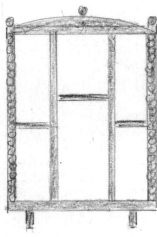

OVERMANTEE

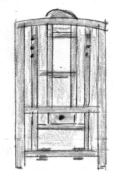

HALL STAND.
UMBERELAS ETC
(SMALL SCALE)

THE TELEVISION
A VERY LATE AD
DITION TO THEM.
REALY BLACK AND
WHITE THEN TO.

G A England 2012.

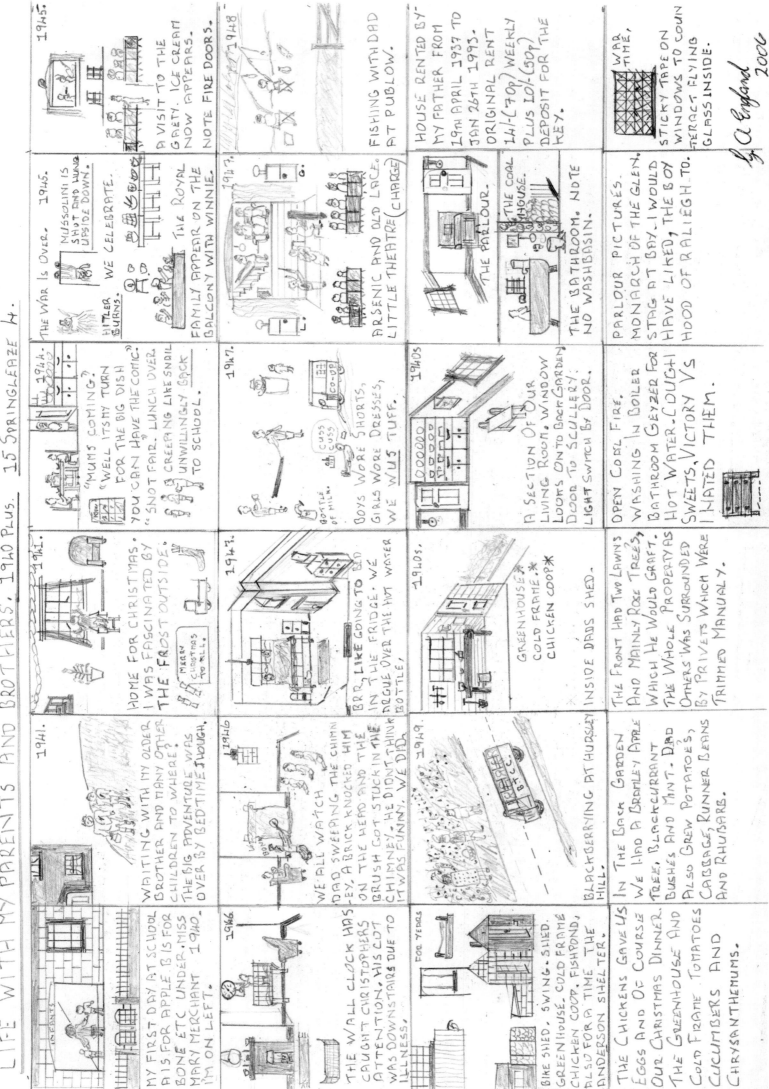

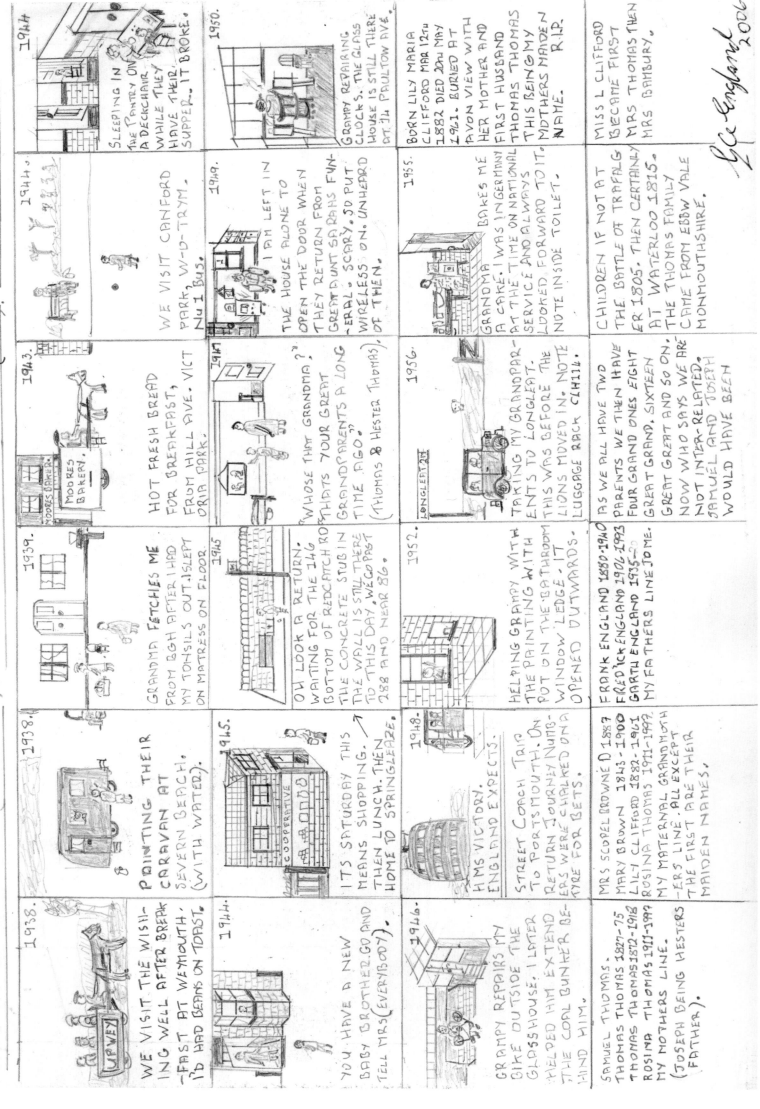

FORMERLY THE GARJULO SCHOOL OF PIANOFORTE. IT ORIGINALY HAD A SINGLE
CENTRAL GATE. THERE WAS NO GARAGE BUT A WELL KEPT GARDEN. IT WAS
RUN BY TWO SISTERS, ELSIE AND GLADYS. MY TUTOR WAS ELSIE AND
HER TWO ASSISTANTS MISS CHITTEY. AND MRS EDWARDS. I WAS A
DISASTER.

I RECALL.

SCHOOL PLAYGROUND.
BOY DID THEY JUMP.
1944.

AGHH-H-H   BOYS

HOME MADE CAP BOMBS.

GRAND NATIONAL 1947

DAD
LOOKS
ON A1.
I CHOOSE.

MY CHOICE CAME 2ND
RON WON £1 AND
GAVE ME 2/6d (12½p).

EVENING SOCIAL 1947
AT MY SCHOOL

2ND PRIZE IN RAFFLE
I CHOSE A LAMPSHADE
FOR MUM.

SHEPHARDS STORE CHRISTMAS 1939
THE POCKET WATCH ON
THE CROCS
TONGUE

HAD A VERY LOUD TICK.

G.A. England 2007

Paperboy 1946–1949

PETHERTON GARDENS.   CIRCA 1936.

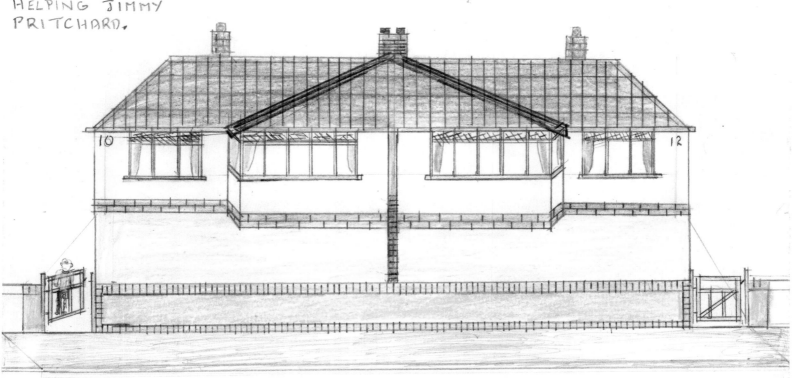

10   12

PART OF. GILDA PARADE 1940s

BLAKE'S   EASTMANS.   NEWS RIGBY CONF   E·A·MITCHELL AND CO

BAKER   BUTCHER   TO   MY 5·0 AM PICKUP POINT.
                           GILDA   1949/50   WINE MERCHANTS.
                           CRES

G A England 2007

PRE-FABS ERECTED 1948 IN AIRPORT RD. KNOWLE.

↑ BROADFIELD RD.

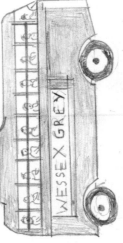

WESSEX GREY

1948 SCHOOL TRIP TO WINDSOR CASTLE.

Ece England 2006.

AS IT IS SATURDAY THERE IS NO SCHOOL SO I AM OUT COLLECT-ING THE PAPER MONEY, IN LONG TROUSERS TO. HOWEVER NOT FOR SCHOOL YET. MY YOUNGEST BRO-THER CHRISTOPHER ACCOMPANIES ME. HE HAS SEEN TWO OTHER BOYS GOING TADPOLING IN THE BROOK AND HAS MOMENTARILY LOST INT-EREST IN ME. JUST AHEAD THOU-GH IS MR MOULDER COLLECTING HIS PEARL ASSURANCE PREMIUMS. HE IS SURE TO WANT SOME CHANGE AND A CHAT. THE AUSTIN SEVEN

COMING UP BEHIND IS PROBABLY MR SINEGAR TAKING HIS MOTHER FOR A DRIVE. THIS CAR CLH114 I WAS TO BUY OF HIM SEVEN YEARS LATER FOR £30. IF YOU HAD A CUSTOMER PAY-ING 2/-(10P) A WEEK IN THOSE DAYS FOR A WEEKS PAPERS YOU HAD A GOOD ORDER, FOR THIS PRINCELY SUM YOU COULD HAVE 6 POSTS, 6 DAILYS, 2 SUNDAYS, A RADIO TIMES AND A GREEN UN PLUS 1d DELIVERY CHARGE. ALSO AT THIS TIME SEVER-AL THOUSAND OF THESE TEMPORARY DWELLINGS WERE IN THE PROCESS OF BEING ERECTED IN THE BRISTOL

AREA. THEY CAME IN TWO HALVES WHICH WERE THEN BOLTED TOGETHER A NOVEL FEATURE BEING A BUILT IN FRIDGE.

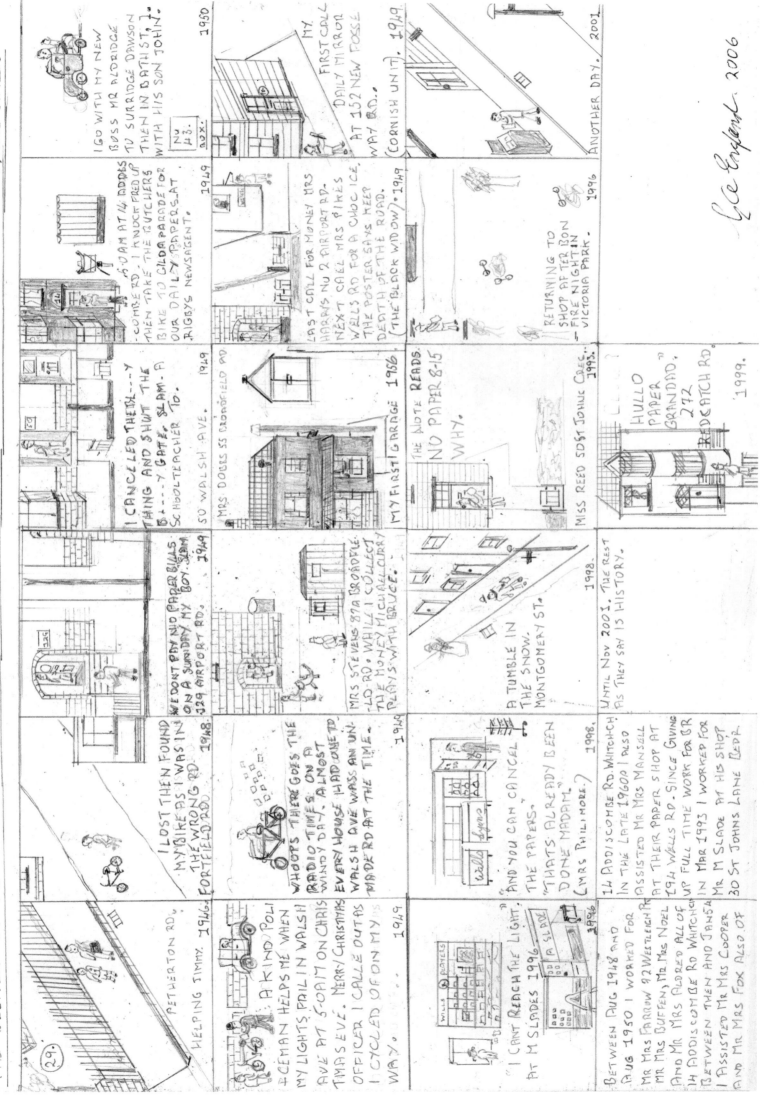

THE DELIVERY OF NEWSPAPERS - LATE FORTIES, COME RAIN OR SHINE, BOTH BEFORE AND AFTER SCHOOL, AND SINCE.

29.

HELPING JIMMY. 1946

PETHERTON RD.

I LOST THEN FOUND MY BIKE AS I WAS IN THE WRONG RD. FORTFIELD RD. 1948

I GO WITH MY NEW BOSS MR ALDRIDGE TO SURRIDGE DAWSON THEN IN BATH ST, WITH HIS SON JOHN. 1950

NU M3. BOX.

5-0 AM AT 14 ADDIS -COMBE RD. I KNOCK FRED UP THEN TAKE THE BUTCHER'S BIKE TO GILDA PARADE FOR OUR DAILY PAPERS, AT RIGBYS NEWSAGENT. 1949

I CANCELLED THEIR ---Y THING, AND SHUT THE B----Y GATE. SLAM. A SCHOOLTEACHER TO. 1949

50 WALSH AVE.

WE DON'T PAY NO PAPER BILLS ON A SUNDAY MY BOY. SLAM. 129 AIRPORT RD. 1948

LAST CALL FOR MONEY MRS HARRIS NU 2 AIRPORT RD. NEXT CALL MRS PIKES WELLS RD FOR A CHOC ICE. THE POSTER SAYS. KEEP DEPTH OF THE ROAD. (THE BLACK WIDOW) 1949

DAILY MIRROR AT 152 NEW FOSSE WAY RD. (CORNISH UNIT) 1949

A KIND POLI -CEMAN HELPS ME WHEN MY LIGHTS FAIL IN WALSH AVE AT 5-0 AM ON CHRIS -TMAS EVE. MERRY CHRISTMAS OFFICER I CALLED OUT AS I CYCLED OF ON MY WAY. 1949

WHOOPS THERE GOES THE RADIO TIMES. ON A WINDY DAY. ALMOST EVERY HOUSE HAD ONE TO WALSH AVE. WAS AN UN-MADE RD AT THE TIME. 1949

MRS DOBBS 55 BROADFIELD RD.

MRS STEVENS 87A BROADFIE -LD. RD. WALL I COLLECT THE MONEY MICHAEL CURRY PLAYS WITH BRUCE. MY FIRST GARAGE 1956

THE NOTE READS. NO PAPER 8-15 WHY.

RETURNING TO SHOP AFTER BON FIRE NIGHT IN VICTORIA PARK. 1996

ANOTHER DAY. 2001

"I CAN'T REACH THE LIGHT." AT M SLADES 1996

WILLS PAPERS

A SLADE

WILLS PAPERS

1996

AND YOU CAN CANCEL THE PAPERS. "THATS ALREADY BEEN DONE MADAM." (MRS PHILLIMORE.) 1998.

A TUMBLE IN THE SNOW. MONTGOMERY ST. 1998.

MISS REED 50 ST JOHNS CRES. 1993.

HULLO PAPER GRANDAD. 272 REDCATCH RD. 1999.

BETWEEN AUG 1948 AND AUG 1950 I WORKED FOR MR MRS FARROW 92 WESTLEIGH RD. ASSISTED MR MRS MANSELL MR MRS BUFFEN, MR MRS NOEL AND MR MRS ALDRED ALL OF 14 ADDISCOMBE RD WHITCHUP BETWEEN THEN AND JAN 5A 14 ADDISCOMBE RD. WHITCH-CH. IN THE LATE 1960S I ALSO AT THEIR PAPER SHOP AT 194 WELLS RD. SINCE GIVING UP FULL TIME WORK FOR BR IN MAR 1993 I WORKED FOR MR M SLADE AT HIS SHOP 30 ST JOHNS LANE BEDM. UNTIL NOV 2001. THE REST AS THEY SAY IS HISTORY.

I ASSISTED MR MRS COOPER AND MR MRS FOX ALSO OF

Ça England. 2006

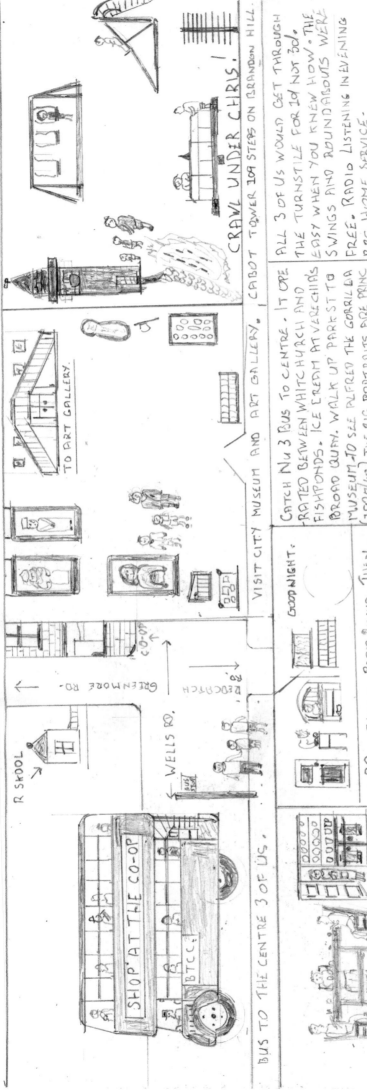

SUNDAY AFTERNOONS LATE 1940's

R SCHOOL
WELLS RD.
GREENMORE RD.
REDCATCH RD.
CO-OP
TO ART GALLERY.
BUS STOP
BTCC?
SHOP AT THE CO-OP

BUS TO THE CENTRE 3 OF US.

CRAWL UNDER CHRIS!

CABOT TOWER 109 STEPS ON BRANDON HILL

VISIT CITY MUSEUM AND ART GALLERY.

ALL 3 OF US WOULD GET THROUGH THE TURNSTILE FOR 1d NOT 3d. EASY WHEN YOU KNEW HOW. THE SWINGS AND ROUNDABOUTS WERE FREE. RADIO LISTENING IN EVENING FREE. BBC HOME SERVICE-
7-30PM-8-30PM VARIETY BANDBOX COMPERED BY DEREK ROY-FRANKIE HOWARD
8-30PM 9-0PM PLAY, THE MAJOR OF CASTERBRIDGE FOR EG. THARDY.
9-0-10-00 PALM COURT. ALBERT SANDLER.

CATCH Nu 3 BUS TO CENTRE. IT OPE -RATED BETWEEN WHITCHURCH AND FISHPONDS. ICE CREAM AT VARIOUS BROAD QUAY. WALK UP PARK ST TO MUSEUM. TO SEE ALFRED THE GORILLA (1927/48) THE BIG PORTRAITS ARE PRINC -ESCARGOD (1789-1864) SHE FOOLED EVERYBODY. AND RAJAH RAM MOHUN ROY (AN INDIAN REFORMER (1774 1833) MARVEL AT OTHER PAINTINGS PARTICULARLY ROLINDA SHARPLES 1794-1838.

GOOD NIGHT.

THINKS, PAPER ROUND THEN SCHOOL, ROLL ON SATURDAY AGAIN. NOTE OLD RADIO LOUD SPEAKER, AND CHAMBER POT UNDER MY BED.

UP AGAIN 4.30 MONDAY MORNING-

ANIMAL, VEGETABLE, OR MINERAL.

WHO CAN CLIMB HIGHEST? ST GERARDS BEFORE THE PRESBITARY WAS BUILT.

A RADIO PROGRAMME THEN.

20? ON THE WAY TO SCHOOL.

A TEST OF NERVES.

SORRY SON BUT ITS AN A.
...ETY CINEMA.

R & J BURNS
J BURNS
SHOES
GREENGROCER
CLEANERS
TOYS KNIT PIGS & COUNTRY

INTEGRAL PART OF THE CINEMA AND OWNED BY MR CHAMBERLAIN. LORD MAYOR ABOUT 1960. THEY WERE IN LATER YEARS INCORPOR -ATED IN THE CINEMA ITSELF.
E.A. England 2006

IN THOSE DAYS SHOPS USUALLY HAD A PORCH WHERE YOU COULD STAND IN THE DRY EVEN IF NOT BUYING. UNLIKE TODAY WHERE EVERY INCH OF FLOOR SPACE IS UTILIZED INSIDE. THESE TWO SHOPS WERE AN

MY CABINET WIND UP GRAMOPHONE 1949. IT PLAYED 78's SUCH AS "THE LAUGHING POLICEMAN" "THE THREE TREE'S" ETC NOT ... OLD WORN OUT ONES MADE USEFULL BULB HOLDERS.

BACK HOME FOR TEA AT 6 OCLOCK-

MON NIGHTS CUBS AND SCOUTS. 137 TROOP-PACK. ST GERARDS.

SKIPPER.
ARKELA.
WEL DIB DIB DIB. WEL DOB DOB DOB.

A SCOUT SMILES AND WHISTLES CHEERFULLY THROUGH ALL DIFFICULT -IES. WE DID TD. OR ELSE.

My Relatives Home
Coloured Yellow.
Uncoloured Portion
Next Doors.

G A England 2010

Down the lane opposite kings-wood park the history of this Georgian property I know not except that the two adjoining cottages were once the servants quarters. The one on the left being once the home of my Aunty May (Florence) and Uncle Wilf Best and my cousins Hazel, Robert (Bobby), Jenifer and Heather. There was a gas supply but not electricity, water but no flush toilet only an outside privvy. It was in the bushes of the big house that I found and was allow -to keep an old radio speaker. It gave me hours of pleasure in my bedroom at Springleaze after I had

taken it home on the bus. The conductor was not very pleased either as it stinked. I cleaned it up and low and behold it worked!. I could listen to it in bed until my parents switched of the Redifusion speaker downstairs, I was then 14 years of age and still at school. My Grandparents old gramophone also gave me much pleasure with a plentifull supply of old 78s to play. In the 1960's the cottages were demolished but the big house remained.

♯ ♪ ♯

G A England 2010

PS. Old disused 78s would make usefull plant pots. This was done by placing them on top of a saucepan of hot steaming water and cloth in hand pressing them down. Depending on the saucepan sides the edges could also be shaped outwards.

MR BURT. KENCHRIS (HOUSE NAME)
43 CALCOTT RD. CIRCA 1935
HEADMASTER WELLS RD 1937/48

MR GRAHAM (JUMBO)
BAYHAM RD CIRCA 1935
HISTORY. (AND THE ROMANS
CAME TO BRITTAIN.).

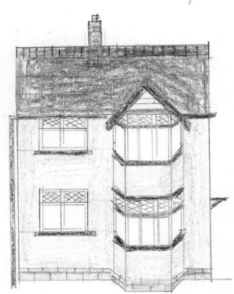

THE MISSES GAY
27 CROWNDALE RD.
CIRCA 1932
ONE, HEADMISSTRESS
OF KNOWLE PARK
SENIOR GIRLS THE
OTHER AN INFANT
SCHOOL TEACHER
OF MINE. SHE
RAPPED MY KNUCKLES
YEARS LATER I
RAPPED HERS (METRICATION)

MR TAYLOR (WHACKER.)
IMPERIAL RD W.
SUCCESSOR TO MR BURT
FROM 1948 "SORY SON HE GOES
YOU STAY!"

G C England 2007

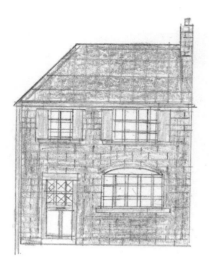

Mr Scully
52 Ponsford Rd
Circa 1932
Lotta Steps.
(Woodwork).

Mr Usher (Cowboy) Metalwork
West Town Lane. "Hurry Up Boy Pick
Circa 1934 .   Your Teeth Up"

Mr Ede
Thiery Rd
Circa 1938
Music And
Geography
Deputy Head.

Mr Hanham
West Town Park.
Circa 1934
Music And Woodwork.

GCEngland 2007

FAMILY HISTORY.

1. HOME OF GT GRANDMA CLIFFORD NARROW PLAIN PRE 1900.
2. HOME OF GRANDMA BAMBURY MONMOUTH ST 1925-31. ST JOHNS LANE.
3. HOME OF GRAMPY FRED BAMBURY ST GABRIELS RD EASTON ABOUT 1910.
4. HOME OF AUNTY ETHEL ST LUKES CRES PRE 1955. (SYMONDS) MUMS COUSIN.
5. HOME OF AUNTY DAISY MIDLAND RD PRE 1952. (TANNER) MUMS COUSIN.
6. HOME OF UNCLE BILL AUNT DAISY NORTH VIEW STAPLE HILL 1930s.
   (DADS OLDER BROTHER).
AN UNUSUAL FEATURE OF No 3. THE WINDOWS OPENED OUTWARDS
DIRECTLY ON TO THE PAVEMENT. GRAMPY FRED WAS MUMS STEPFATHER.
A BOOTSCRAPERS. ALL EXCEPT No 5 WOULD HAVE HAD AN OUTSIDE
TOILET AND NO BATHROOM.
No's 1 AND 3 DEMOLISHED AROUND 1966.

G A England 2008

Telegram Boy 1950–1953

BROKEN LINES INDICATE WAR
DAMAGE BY INCENDIARY BOMBS 1941/2
TELEGRAPH DELIVERY PHONE 21837.

HELD IN OFFICE

KELLYS
DIRECTOR
1946

W.H
M.W
6d
6d

TELEGRAMS 1/6d PER DOZ
WAKELYNS WORDS EXTRAS 1d EACH
STREET GUIDE
FROM ANY
NEWSAGENT.

POST OFFICE.

1 2 3 4 5

WITTS
BREAD

OUT
OF
BOUNDS
TO BOYS.
↓
LIFT

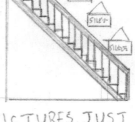

GPO

GPO

TELEGRAPH DELIVERY.
AS REG MAKES THE TEA
IN OUR LOCKER/REST ROOM
FRED IS BUSY IN HIS OF
-FICE. TWO BOYS SIT
WAITING FOR WORK AS
TWO OTHERS GO OUT
AND ONE RETURNS AS
OUR CAKES ETC ARRIVE.
ONE FLOOR UP, ALONG
THE PASSAGE ALTHOUGH
YOU ARE STILL IN THE
BUILDING A DOOR LEADS
TO THE OPEN AIR DUE
TO BOMBING 8 OR SO
YEARS BEFORE.
PINK DOCKET, UNABLE TO LEAVE
YELLOW DOCKET, LEFT WITH NEIGH+R.
-BOUR.

AND
OPPOSITE.
↓

GEORGES BEERS.

GEORGES

THE OTHER
ASSIZE COURT.
17TH CENTURY.

NOT PICTURES JUST
ONE WORD SILENCE.

THE ASSIZE COURT
IS NEXT DOOR AND A
BOY CAN BE NOISY.
WHEN BORED.

IN THE CANTEEN
BEVERAGES OR SOFT
DRINKS ONLY. BUT
CAKES, CRISPS,
AND BREAD ROLLS
FOR SUBSIDIZED MEALS
WE'D GO TO THE GEN-
ERAL CANTEEN UPSTAI
-RS. SITTING AWAY
FROM ADULT STAFF.
NO 1455.

G A England 2010

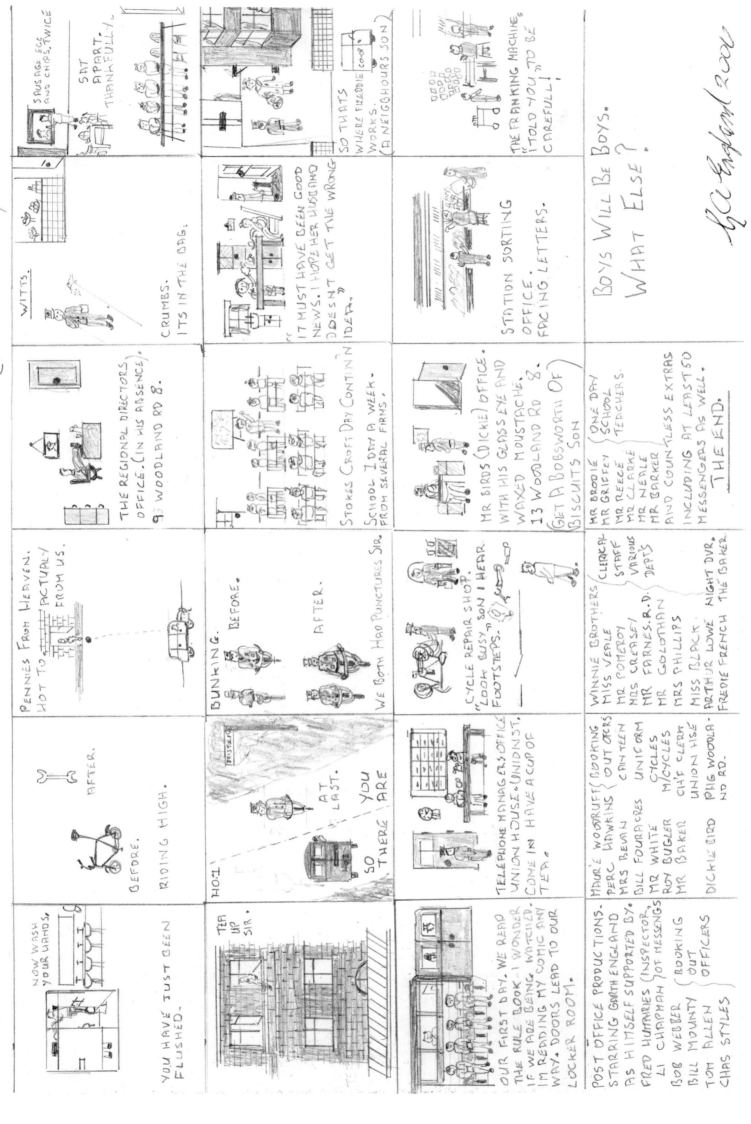

Soldier 1954–1956

BRISTOL T MEADS. 14.

21ST JAN 1954. GOODBYE FOR A MONTH. ON A 48 HR PASS. BY THE TIME I GOT HOME. IT WAS VIRTUALLY TIME TO GO BACK. 8.0AM

RICHMOND. MR.

7.0PM. CLIMB ABOARD LADS YOUR IN THE ARMY NOW. JUMP TO IT THEN. YOU NEXT LADDIE.

A.W.O.L. BY THE LEFT HWK MUCH OW OW/OW 1E-OW.

THIS CHAP HAD ASKED FOR COMPASSIONATE LEAVE AS HIS WIFE WAS EXPECT -ING. IT WAS REFUSED. THEY TREATED HIM AS THO -UGH HE WAS A CRIMINAL.

DRILLING IN THE SNOW. SGT GRAY SNOWBALL IN HAND.

TESTING YOUR STAMINA. JUMP UP AND HANG ON. CHARGE THEN JUMP. CPL OUTFIELD.

GUARD DUTY. BOURLON LINES. ESCAPEES ON ROOF.

WVS. WOMENS VOLUNTARY SERVICES.

QM STORES. SGMS SAGU. SIGN YUR. NEXT UN ONEE. (NO DAILY MIRRORS TODAY CHAPS.) RIFLE RANGE

COOKHOUSE.

IN THE NAAFI

ON FATIGUES. SPURS IN / SPURS OUT / PANTRY

THE COCKNEY WRAC CPL HAS LEFT THE PANTRY DOOR UNLOCKED. BE QUICK. CHEESE CORN BEEF AND CURRANTS. TO HAND.

ARMOURED COMPANY VEHICLE. ACV

OPEN TOILETS AT RHEINDAHLEN. W. GERMANY.

ADMIN OFFICE. BARRACK SQUARE.

CAUGHT BORROWING SGT CURRY BIKE. "IL HAVE YOUR B----Y LIFE BLOOD LADDIE."

PAY PARADE.

EVERY THURS. WHEN YOUR NAME IS CALLED STEP SMARTLY FORWARD SALUTE THE OFFICER GIVE YOUR NAME RANK AND NUMBER SALUTE AGAIN SMART ABOUT TURN MARCH OF - BERRET TO HAVE BEEN REMOVED. DEF -ORE. IF ON A CHARGE.

MEDICAL OFFICER MO ROLL YOUR SLEEVE UP.

YOU COULD REFUSE BUT IT WOULD BE YOUR RESPONSIBIL -ITY. IF YOU WERE SENT TO THE OTHER SIDE OF THE WORLD AND BECAME ILL.

RHQ. RQMS

PERSONEL REGIMENTAL INSTITUTES WHERE FRAU ME WOULD SELL YOU A NICE GIFT TO TAKE HOME. ON RETIREMENT FRAU YONGE TOOK OVER. NICE LADIES TO BOUNDS.

NOT FORGETTING THREE TELEPRINTER FRAULINES, ZEIGE, KLIENE, AND OF COURSE MARLISE. TWO CYPHER CORPORALS IAN SYKES AND GEORGE SHEPH -ARD. LT DAVENPORT EX ANSON CHURCH ARMY. RSM. MAJOR COLLINSON SGT MAJORS SWANN AND ERRIDGE. THE PADRE. LCPL FOX.

HERMAN THE GERMAN. DRIVER. SGMS DUNLOP SGTS FOSTER, GIBBS, SMITH, SEVERN. CPLS ELLIS AND BRACEY AND EVER SO MANY SQUADDIES. CAPTAIN MOTTO CIRTA CETO (SWIFT AND SURE).

THE MSO THATS MIXED SERVICE ORGANIZATION BEING DISPLACED PEOPLE FROM THE SECOND WORLD WAR.

BAFSV THATS BRITISH ARM -ED SERVICE VOUCHER. OUR CURRENCY WAS NOT ALLOWED EXCEPT COPPER SO WE HAD PAPER £5.1T 2/- 2/6d -10s- AND £1. DEUTCH MARKS COULD BE OBTAINED AT PAY PARADE. THEIR EXCHANGE RATE BEING 11.82d. USE-

-FULL FOR SAT NIGHTS IN PADERBORN. SERVED WITH COFFEE CHRISTMAS MORNING. LACED WITH RUM BY SENIOR NCOS. THE ONLY TIME OF YEAR. REGIMENTAL MARCH BEGONE DULL CARE. ARMY BOOK 64. PARTS ONE AND TWO.

GCE England 2000

PADERBORN DIE RATHOUSE. THE TOWN HALL IN ENGLISH.

CLIFTON DOWN.

THE BRIDGE HOUSE.

CIRCA 1840.

A1. YOU ARE IN MY SON.
(DEC 1953). HAPPY CHRISTMAS!
SERVICE MEDICALS TOOK PLACE HERE
PAY 4/- A DAY £1.40p A WEEK.

MESS TINS.

PINT MUG.

EATING IRONS.

ARMY BED PACK.

BLANCO.

AFN
ARMY FORM
AFO.
BLANK.

217 ROS3
ENGLAND

PACK UP YOUR TROUBLES.

BUTTON STICK AND HOUSWIFE.

"HOW LONG HAVE YOU BEEN IN THE ARMY SON? ALL DAY SIR."
"IF IT MOVES SALUTE IT, IF IT DON'T PAINT IT.

OUR COL IN CHIEF
THE PRINCESS ROYAL.

CLIFTON SUSPENSION BRIDGE.

Joe England 2008.

6.0 AM WAKEY WAKEY
7.0 AM BREAKFAST
8.0 AM GET FELL IN
10.30 AM NAAFI BREAK
MID DAY LUNCH
1.0 PM GET FELL IN
5.0 PM TEA. THEN
KIT CLEANING.
7.0 PM NAAFI OR
CHURCH ARMY
10.0 PM GET THOSE
BLOODY LIGHTS OUT
CAMP CINEMA WHEN
FREE. NO LEAVING
BEFORE NATIONAL
ANTHEM OR ELSE.
ALSO WVS CLUB.

MRS WILBERFORCE LIVES HERE
ALONE. UNTIL FOUR DUBIOUS
GENTLEN ARRIVE LOOKING
FOR ROOMS TO RENT.
(THE LADY KILLERS.)

G.A. England
2013

1956. A New Begining   My First Car.   CLH 114.

There Was Also A Slightly Larger Version, It Was Known As The Big Seven.

An Erlier Version Of The Two Was Nicknamed The Corned Beef Tin.

A 1935 Austin Seven Ruby Saloon 7 H Power Purchased Of Of Mr George

Bernard Sinigar Of Davids Rd Hengrove In The Summer Of 1956 For The Sum

Of £30. It Had Spoked Wheels, A Running Board (Two), Cable Brakes,

Starting Handle And A Luggage Rack. At That Time One Rear Light Was

The Norm As Were Direction Arm Indicators. Petrol Cost 4/6d (22½p) Per

Gallon Tax And Ins Would Set You Back £25 Per Year. No Traffic Wardens,

Parking Metres Or Yellow Lines. When Not Required The Luggage Rack

Would Simply Fold Up Under The Spare Wheel Cover. A Puncture Repair

Cost Usualy 5/- (25p). Happy Motoring? Most Definately. Also No MOT.

It Even Had A Transomed Windscreen. CLH 114.   G A England 2006

No Breathalizer. Simply Walk In A Straight Line Or Else.

Milkman 1958–1976

A E TOZER & ROGER.

MY FIRST PAY.
£3 FOR TWO DAYS.
"WHATS THE MATTER
SON ISN'T ?"
IT ENOUGH?
AT MY
REPLY HIS
GLASSES FELL OFF.
(IT WAS MORE THAN I
EXPECTED.

FLOAT GARAGES TALBOT RD.
THIS WOULD HAVE BEEN
THE GARDEN OF THE HOUSE
IN PRIORY RD WHERE QUEEN
ELIZABETH 1ST IS REPUTED
TO HAVE SLEPT.
✳ MINE.

FROM A PHOTOGRAPH TAKEN BY MASTER
ALAN MATHEWS AGED 11 OF 18 TENNIS
RD SUMMER 1960. (BRAGCHURCH). IN
REALITY ROMAN LETTERS AND NUMBERS
WERE USED. ON FLEET ETC.

1961/2
BLACK ICE EVERYWHERE

1962/3
HELP, HELP.
BOTH AT LANGHAM RD KNOWLE.
HOLD THE WALL. YOU MUST BE JOKING.
SNOW SNOW THICK THICK SNOW

YOUR LATE   YOUR EARLY.

49   51

NEIGHBOURS DISPUTE OVER
GARAGE ROOFS IN STONELEIGH CRES
"NOW WE CANT PAINT OUR FENCE,
AND HAVENT SPOKEN FOR 20 YEARS."
STRINGER/TURNER.

MILKMAN
MY WIFE
HAS JUST
HAD A BABY,
PLEASE LEAVE
ANOTHER ONE.
WERE HAVING SOME
FRIENDS FOR LUNCH.
MY REPLY "WELL I
HOPE YOU ENJOY EM"

TOOLS OF THE TRADE.

ROUNDBOOK
AND PENCIL
HANDCRATE, CHURN, HOOK, LADLE,
NB IT BECAME ILLEGAL TO SELL LOOSE
MILK FROM THE CHURN IN 1950.
ALSO CARDBOARD, TOPS WERE REPLACED
BY TINFOIL AND ½PINTS OBSOLETE.

"GER OFF

YOU DONT KNOW
WHERE IVE BEEN."

ITS NO GOOD
CRYING OVER

SPILT MILK.

"THIS MILKS SOUR"
MRS DUDRIDGE
22 ROOKERY RD.
THIS IN 6 FEET OF
SNOW AND SUB
ZERO TEMPERATURES.
I ENDED UP WITH A BLOB
OF IT ON MY NOSE.

THE TREE THAT SAVED ME. AT
THE CORNER OF CALCOTT RD
SEPT 1969.
PHONE BOX
NEARBY TO.

"COME ON GO FOR

UNCLE ROGER.
OVERNIGHT THE BATY
-WAS PINCHED.

USEFULL IN THE DAIRY
UNTIL THE CONSTANT
STEAM MELTED THE
GLUE HOLDING ITS
WOODEN CASING
TOGETHER. MY WELL
INTENDED GIFT WAS
THEN NO MORE -ORIG
INALY MY STEPFATHERS

THAT DARN CAT.
ALSO
STONE
LEIGH
CRES NU
52. AS
THE LADY
WATCHES
COYLEY
FROM
BEHIND THE
CURTAIN.

MILK
MARKETTING
BOARD.
ONE EXTRA PINTA PLEASE

COLLAR TO BOOST
SALES. EARLY SIXTIES.
MRS CLOTHIER 16 TENNIS RD

VALE ST TOTTERDOWN.
1963 WITH ROGER NASH

"GO CAREFULL SON"
BUT NO NOT HE.

AND ES.ME ABOVE AT 216
STRATFORD HOUSE →

200A WELLS RD.

BEATIE
FLORRIE
EVA
ELSIE AND
AGNES
BLESS EM.

FISH & CHIPS

LITTLE OLD LADIES (5)
EVERYWHERE AT 200A.
(PICTURE OF WINSTON CHURCHILL).

AS BEATIE TIDYS HER HAIR,
FLORRIE HAS A CUP OF TEA.
EVA WAITS AT THE DOOR,
ELSIE HAS JUST ARRIVED.
AS AGNES IS OTHERWISE ENGAGED,
AND I ARRIVE WITH THE MILK.

G.C.England 2007

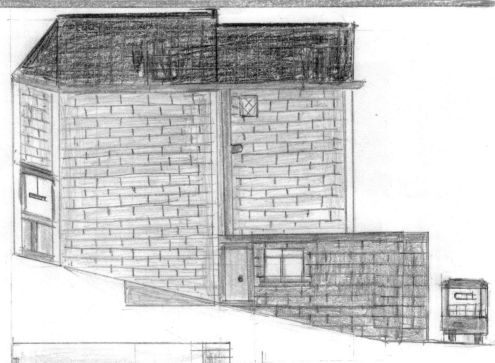

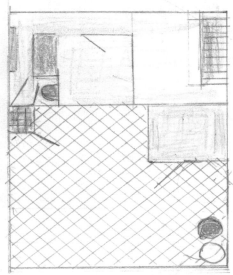

FRONTAGE
SIDE VIEW
REAR VIEW
CELLAR & DAIRY
GROUND FLOOR
FIRST FLOOR
ATTIC

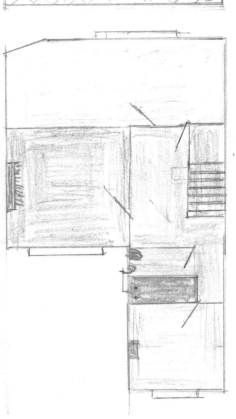

G A England 2012

H. Hucker and Son Fairseat Farm Chew Stoke.

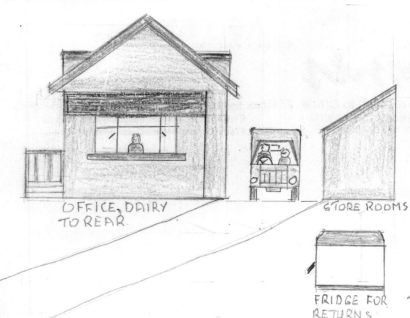

OFFICE, DAIRY TO REAR.

STORE ROOMS

FRIDGE FOR RETURNS

SITUATED ON BREACH HILL. ERNEST AND MARGARET AND THEIR CHILDREN ANTHONY AND GERALDINE LIVED NEARBY IN THE RETREAT WHERE JOHN WESLEY HAD PREACHED. WHILE ANNE IS BUSY IN THE OFFICE. YOUNG MIKE HAS COME FOR A RIDE. IN 1974 HUCKERS PASSED ONTO CLIFFORDS. PREVIOUS TO THIS IN 1970 TOZERS WENT TO UNIGATE THE REST AS THEY SAY IS HISTORY.

MOTOR FUELS

WORKSHOP.

Jubilee Rd Dairy

37 JUBILEE RD KNOWLE WAS FROM 1908/9 A TEMPORARY RC CHURCH. AQUIRED BY ALBERT AROUND 1930 HE GRADUALY BUILT UP A THRIVING DAIRY BUSINESS. AT ITS CLOSURE IN 1970 HE WAS PROCESSING DAILY ABOUT 500 GALLONS OF MILK FOR DAILY DOORSTEP DELIVERY SEVEN DAYS A WEEK. HE REALY HAD A MARVELOUS WORK CAPACITY RETIRING WHEN HE WAS 68 YEARS OF AGE. PREVIOUS OWNER A MR PETHERBRIDGE.

G C England 2012

RUMBLE 114 CHARLTON RD
KEYNSHAM. CIRCA 1952.
SCHOOLMATE DAVID.

MANTZ 6A PONSFORD RD.
CIRCA 1960. MILK ROUND
HELPERS BROTHERS WILLIAM
AND BRIAN.

NASH 18 BRECKNOCK RD.
CIRCA 1905. MILK ROUND
HELPER FOR SIX YEARS ROGER.

HARRIS 25 NEWQUAY RD.
CIRCA 1932. MILK ROUND
HELPER MICHAEL.

CIRCA 1870.

BIBLE PUNCHING BESSIE
HILLSIDE TERRACE
TOTTERDOWN.
"I'M A SICK WOMAN."
(CUSTOMER).

ACE TAXI'S
205 WELLS RD
(CUSTOMER).
CIRCA 1890

2007

OAP 2000–2014

288 Redcatch Rd.

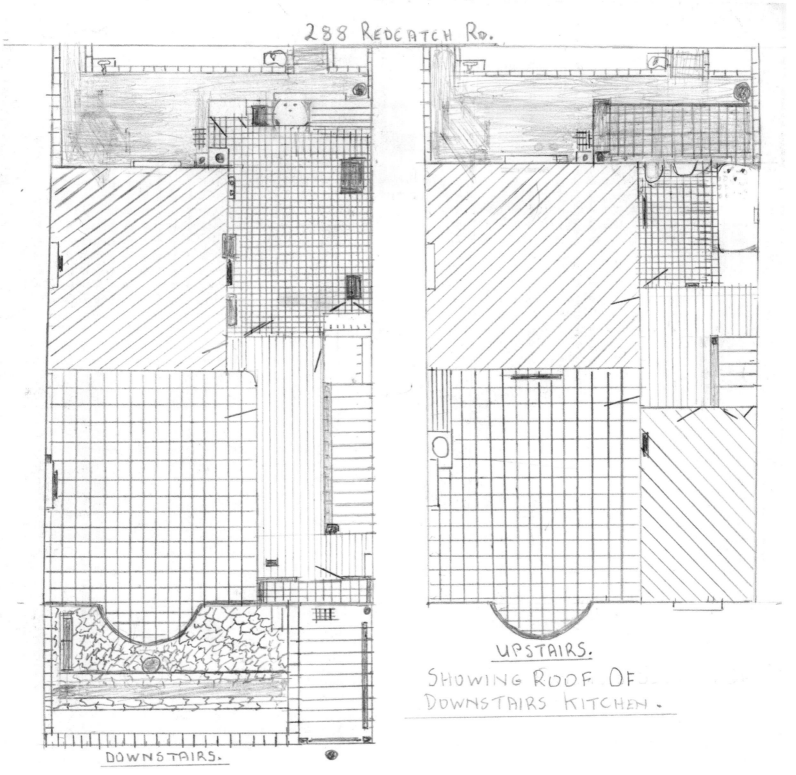

DOWNSTAIRS.

UPSTAIRS.
SHOWING ROOF OF
DOWNSTAIRS KITCHEN.

It Was The Steps Wot Dunit. Due To The Sudden Death Of My Mothers
Second Husband With Her Help I Purchased The Above Property For The Sum
Of £3800 For Security For Us Both In The Future. That Future Is Now
The Present For Me As Mother Has Passed On. And I Have No Other Dependants.
In Poor Health Myself Now I Feel That I Did The Right Thing And Am Quite
Settled And Content At HENGROVE LODGE. My First Monthly Rep-
Was £21/4s/10d. (£21/24) At Redcatch Rd. GCEngland 2006

PLAN OF UPSTAIRS HENGROVE LODGE.

NOW AND THEN.

CIRCA 1925.

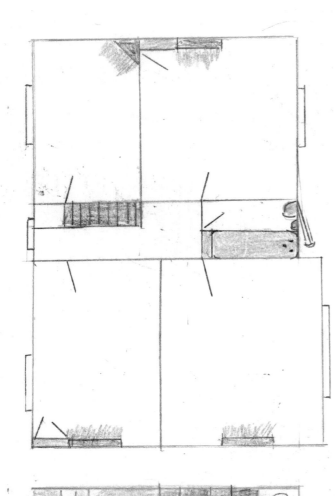

Room 4.

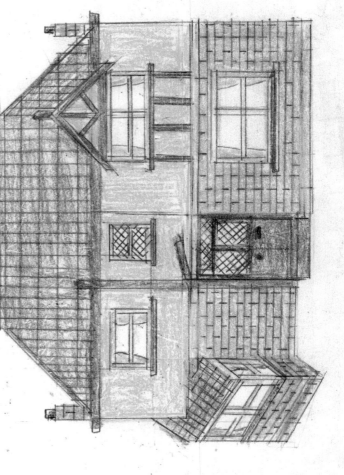

HENGROVE LODGE BUILT FACING
PETHERTON RD AND THE OTHER WAY
AROUND. THUS STILL GIVING AN
UNINTERUPTED VIEW ACROSS OPEN
COUNTRY IN 1925. THE SPEEDWAY/
GREYHOUND RACING TRACK WAS
YET TO BE IN 1928. WOULD HAVE
BEEN ENHASED BY AN OUTSIDE
PORCH, AND LEVEL FLOOR UPSTAIRS.

Gc England 2013

PLAN OF GROUND FLOOR HENGROVE LODGE. (OBSERVATION AND IMAGINATION)

LA England 2013

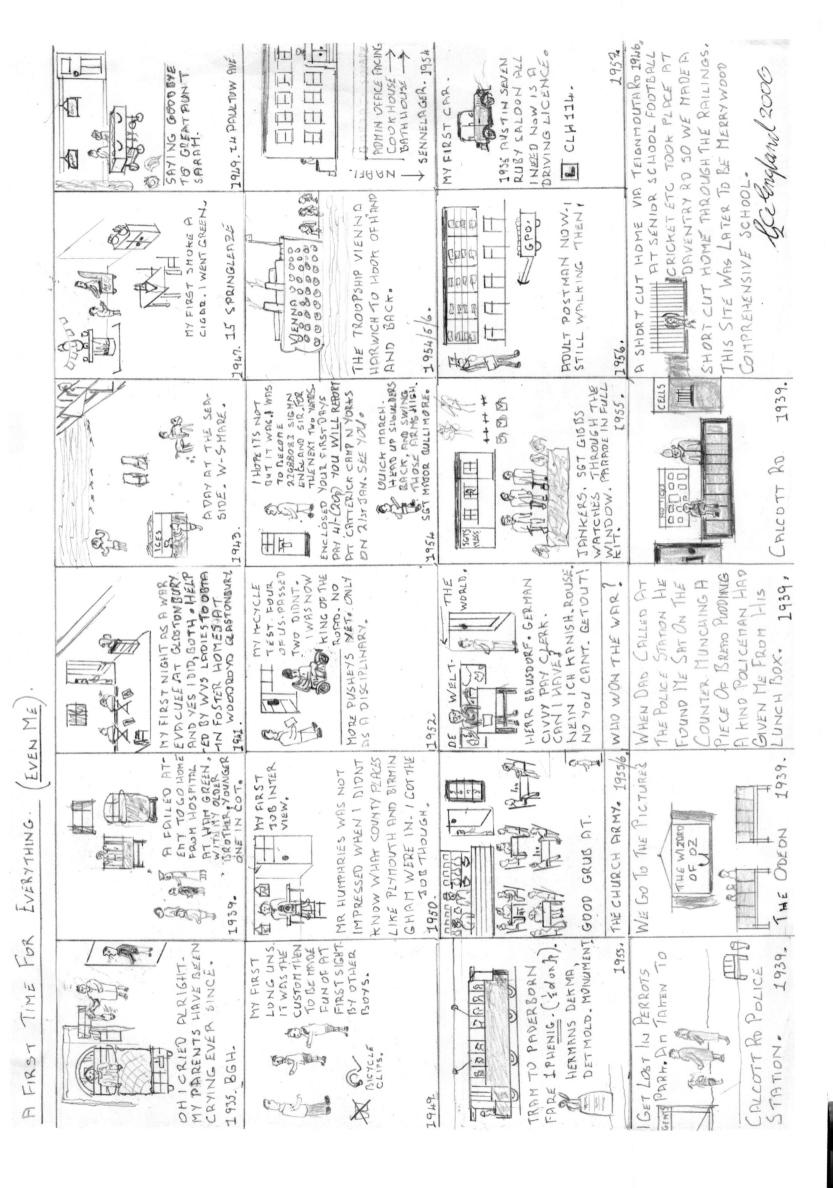

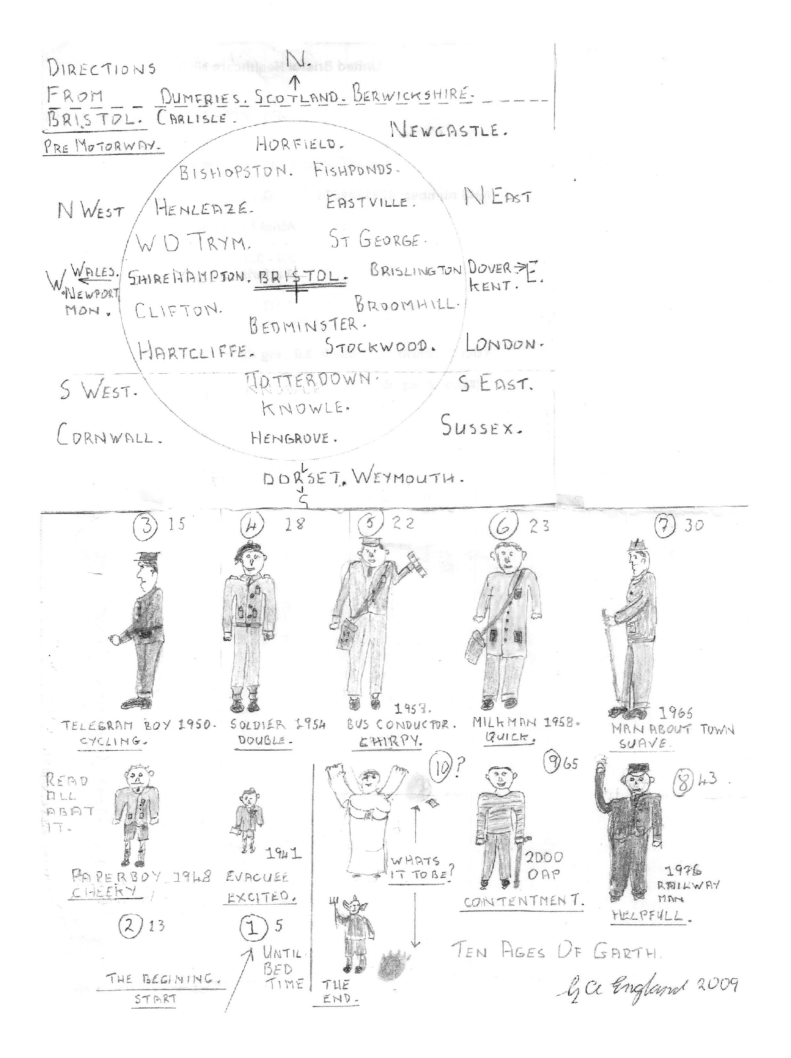

DIRECTIONS
FROM ___ DUMFRIES. SCOTLAND. BERWICKSHIRE. _____
BRISTOL. CARLISLE.
                                    NEWCASTLE.
PRE MOTORWAY.   HORFIELD.

        BISHOPSTON. FISHPONDS.

N WEST. HENLEAZE.   EASTVILLE.   N EAST

    W D TRYM.   ST GEORGE.

W WALES. SHIREHAMPTON. BRISTOL.   BRISLINGTON DOVER →E
  NEWPORT   KENT.
 MON.   CLIFTON.   BROOMHILL.

            BEDMINSTER.
    HARTCLIFFE.   STOCKWOOD.   LONDON.

            TOTTERDOWN.
S WEST.   S EAST.
            KNOWLE.

CORNWALL.   HENGROVE.   SUSSEX.

        DORSET. WEYMOUTH.
                S

③ 15   ④ 18   ⑤ 22   ⑥ 23   ⑦ 30

TELEGRAM BOY 1950.   SOLDIER 1954   BUS CONDUCTOR.   MILKMAN 1958.   MAN ABOUT TOWN
CYCLING.   DOUBLE.   CHIRPY.   QUICK.   SUAVE.
                                   1957.   1965

READ   ⑩?   1976
ALL   ⑨65   RAILWAY
ABAT   1941   MAN
IT.   WHATS   2000
                                       IT TO BE?   OAP   ⑧ 43
PAPERBOY 1948 EVACUEE   CONTENTMENT.   HELPFULL.
CHEEKY   EXCITED.
② 13   ① 5   TEN AGES OF GARTH.
                   UNTIL
THE BEGINING.   BED
   START   TIME   THE   G E England 2009
                           END.

Local Buildings

I Heard Queen Elizabeth 1st Slept Here Once.

KNOWLE HOUSE.

This Property Was Once On The Corner Of Priory Rd — Talbot Rd. It Was Demolished 1953 For Modern Housing. (Drawn From Memory.!)

RED LION HILL   ROSE COTTAGE ST MARTINS RD.   CIRCA 1859.

ONE OF A RANK BUILT 1953.

ADJOING ROSE COTT -AGE WAS THE REAR ENTRANCE FOR BEER'S ETC OF THE RED LION.

G A England 2007

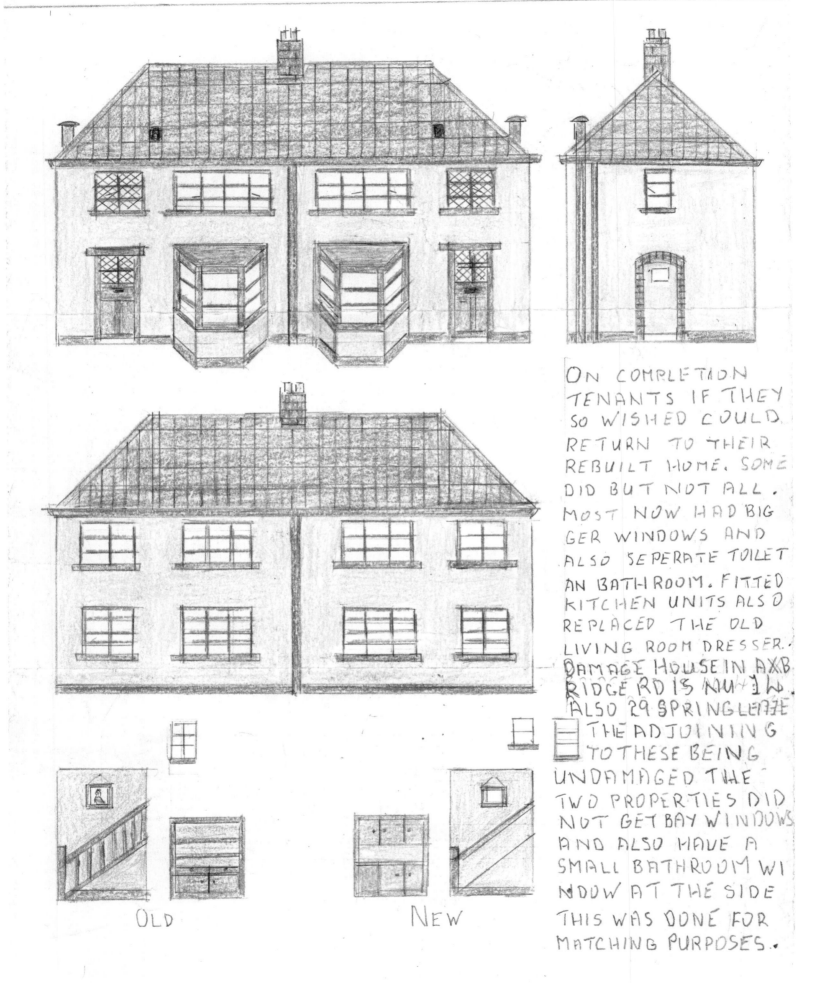

Old   New

On completion
tenants if they
so wished could.
return to their
rebuilt home. some
did but not all.
most now had big
ger windows and
also seperate toilet
an bathroom. fitted
kitchen units also
replaced the old
living room dresser.
Damage house in Axb
ridge rd is no+iw.
also 29 springleaze
the adjoining
to these being
undamaged the
two properties did
not get bay windows
and also have a
small bathroom wi
ndow at the side
this was done for
matching purposes.

G A England 2012.

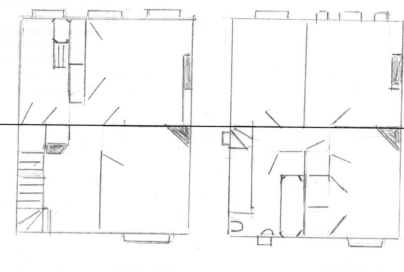

WAR DAMAGED WAKEFIELD
TYPE.

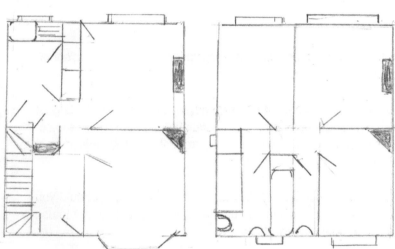

REBUILT 1946.
BATH AND WC
NOW SEPERATE.
AND ALSO REBUILT
WITH FRONT BAY
WINDOW. SCALE
USED SMALLER THAN
ILUSTRATIONS. ALSO
KITCHEN UNITS REP
LACING LIVING ROOM
DRESSER.

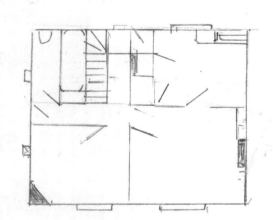

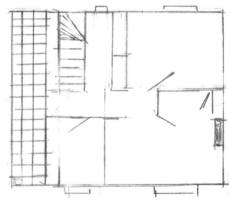

TANK TYPE.
I THINK THAT
THIS TYPE ON
REBUILDING NOW
HAVE AN EXTA
TOILET IN THE
FORMER COAL
HOUSE. COAL NOW
BEING KEPT IN
A STORE UNDER
THE INTERIOR
STAIRCASE DOOR
OF COURSE OUTSIDE.

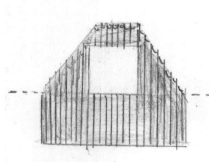

STONGLY MADE OF
REINFORCED COROGATED
STEEL THEY SAVED MANY
LIVES. DOORLESS COLD
AND DARK. SORT THAT
OUT YOURSELVES, YOU
COULD COVER THE SIDES
WITH UP TO A FOOT OF
SOIL AND GROW FLOWERS
ETC. BROKEN LINES IND
ECATE GROUND LEVEL.

R A England 2012

ON THE CORNER OF
SCHOOL RD THE HOME
OF DR MARY EASBY.
DEMOLISHED EARLY 1960s.
(Nu 170 ?)

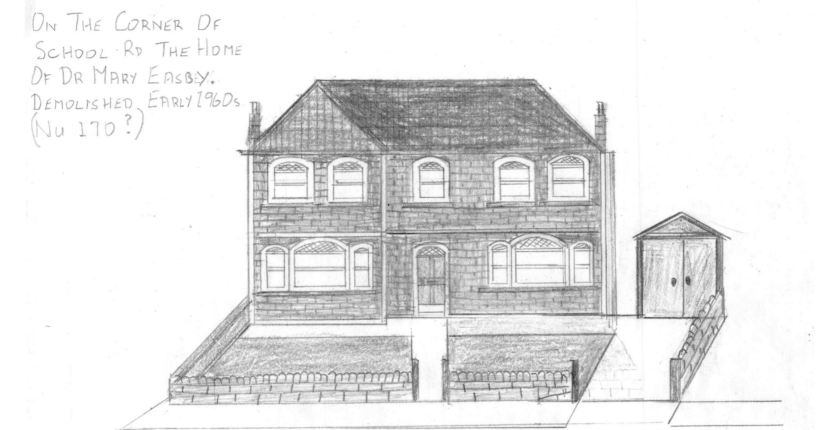

FROM MEMORY
DR LUCAS
184? WELLS RD.
NOW A WINE
SHOP BUT PREVIOUSLY
A FURNITURE SHOP.
ALSO CIRCA 1880.

COTTAGES CLYDE RD.

29 ARNOS ST
TOTTERDOWN.
THE HOME OF
GT AUNT SARAH.
AFTER SHE WAS
BOMBED OUT IN
ST LUKES RD.

29 WILKI
NSON   R S GUY   23 SWEET?

G England 2007

SUDENLY IT IS
RAINING.

FORTFIELD RD.

MISS U CROOK
FORTFIELD RD.
CIRCA 1965.
(U FOR URSULA
HONEST).
LANE AT SIDE
TO ASDA

G A England 2007

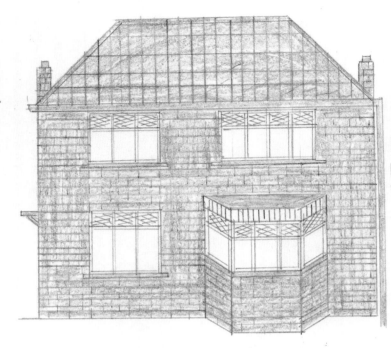

Greatly Enlarged
Right Hand Side.
Upstairs Exterior
Now Faced. Bay
Also To Left.

Taite.
Circa 1920.

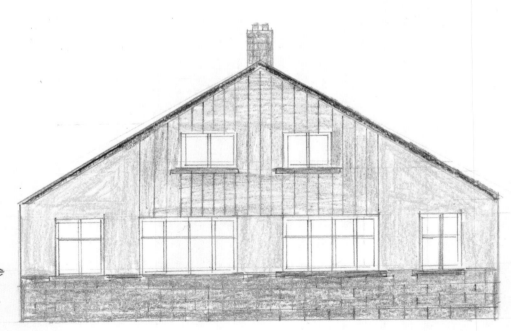

670C →

A and B
←

Worgan
670D
Circa 1965

Newsagent At Newquay Rd.

G A England 2007

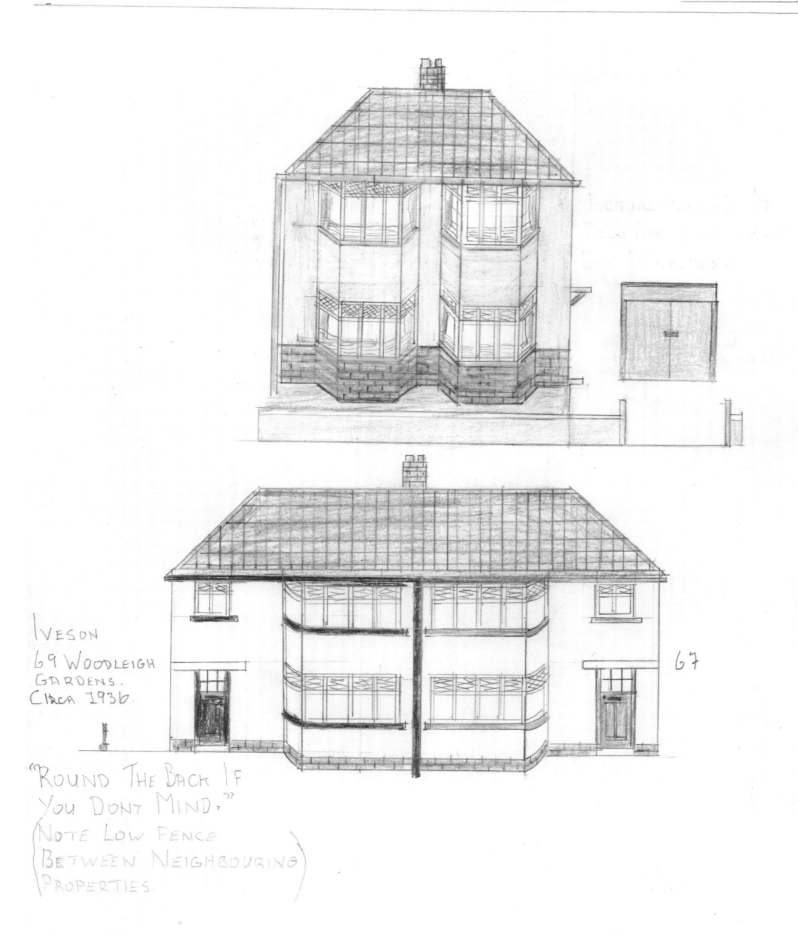

Iveson
69 Woodleigh
Gardens.
Circa 1936.

67

"Round The Back If
You Dont Mind,"
(Note Low Fence
(Between Neighbouring)
Properties.

E. A. England 2007

Wells Rd Knowle.

Popular Victorian Villas

Circa 1890

334

336 Mr Mrs Daniels

338 The Misses Eliot

How Dare You Put That My Wife ... Leaflet in My Door.

P.A England 2013

← St Agnes Ave.   Rookery Rd.   Bayham Rd. →

Gould. 48.   Perry. 46.   Scott. 44.   Evans. 42 Domus.

Mason 75   Delahaye 73.   Lee's 71.   Slocombe 69.   Burnett. 67

Seen From
Tennis Rd

← Maesknoll Rd →

Down Garden Path.

P A England 2008

49　51　-53　　　　　　55　　　　57　　　　59

46　　　　　　　　　　　　　　　　　54

REAR OF 48 ROOKERY RD　　50. SMITH.　　　　52.

HOME TO THE GOULD (4 BOYS) GEOFREY MARTIN STEPHEN ANDREW

FAMILY. FROM REAR UPST　　B 1947　1949　1951　1959.

-AIRS FANTASTIC VIEWS　　ARTISTIC LICENSE AT REAR.

ACROSS THE CITY ARE

TO BE SEEN. CIRCA 1934.

46 PERRY.
50 SMITH.
52 ?
54 ?
49 SMITH.
51 DAY.
53 ? A VICAR.
55 BOND.
57 HARRIS.
59 JONES.

NEARBY A
DESIRABLE
BUNGALOW
23 BAYHAM RD

→

INTERIER
IMAGINED.

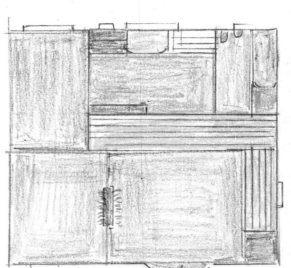

MY FAVOURITE ROAD KNOWLE. GCi England 2008.

Q. HOW DO THE BATH BUSES RUN MATE
A. ON WHEELS THE SAME AS THE REST OF EM.

FORMERLY BRISTOL TRAMWAYS AND CARRIAGE CO.

ST GERARDS RC CHURCH CIRCA 1909.
FR BARRY.   FR REA.

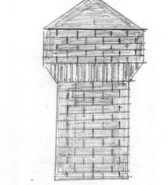

KNOWLE WATER TOWER
CIRCA 1905.

G A England 2007

HERE AT ST MICHAEL AND ALL ANGELS IN 1928 MY MATERNAL GRANDMOTHER LILY MARIA THOMAS NEE CLIFFORD ENTERED INTO HER SECOND MARRIAGE TO FREDERICK ORCHARD BAMBURY OF ST GABRIELS RD EASTON. UNTIL 1931 THEY LIVED AT 19 MONMOUTH ST THEN MOVED TO 14 PAULTOW AVE. HERE IN APRIL 1990 I ATTENDED A MEMORIAL SERVICE FOR A WORKMATE GEORGE DAVIS. HE HAD BEEN KILLED WHILE CYCLING TO WORK TO DO MY NIGHTSHIFT.

G.C.England 2008

Nos 1-3-5 Sylvia Ave Lower Knowle   Circa 1932

Side Window
← Looked
Straigh At 13
Bayham Rds
Front Door.

CLIFTON VIEW
COGGINS

TOWER VIEW
PARR

GLENTHORNE
TOZER

MYRTLE
DENE.
DAVIS

23 Bayham Rd.   Circa 1934.

Integral garage
A later addition of
1960s. Another Nice
Choice For Retirement.

Rookery Rd.

Once Home To A
District Nurse.
(Retired).

Round The Back
For Cleaners.

G A England 2006

St Johns Lane To St Lukes Rd 1 → St Johns Lane.

Circa 1918.

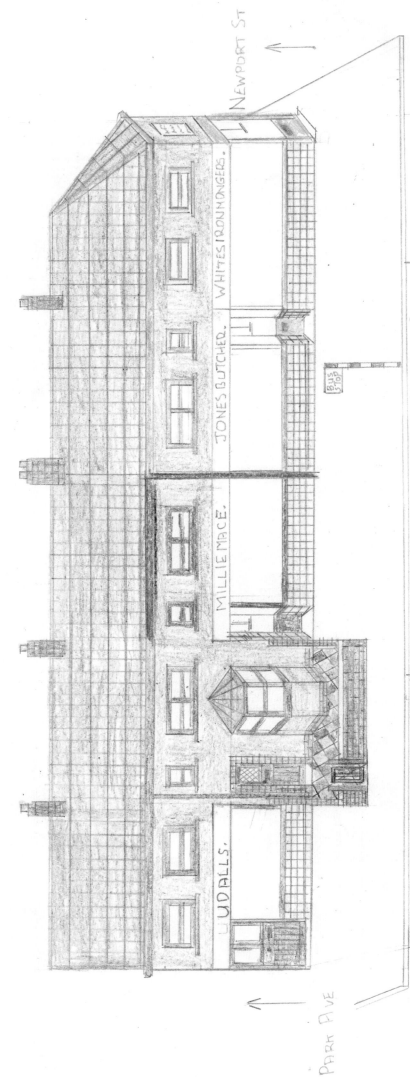

Park Ave

Newport St

Probably Only The End Two Premises
Built As Shops. The Middle Three As
Private Housing. Uddalls Was A
Cycle Shop With A Commercial Garage
At The Rear And Their Living Acc
—omodation Next Door Whilst
Whites Later Became Telebond.
At The Bus Stop You Could Catch The
146 Single Decker To Prince St Or The
20 (Double) To Clyde Rd Redland.

On the opposite side you found a Baptist
Church, Butcher, Post Office, Green
Grocer, Doctor And A Wool Shop Bet
ween Many Private Houses Built About
1930.

G C Enfield 2007

BUNGALOW WINGFIELD RD. CIRCA 1960.

BEWARE OF
THE DOG.

THE WEDGE ST PETERS RISE · HEADLEY PARK. CIRCA 1965

A HOUSE OF
MANY STEPS.

GA Enford 2007

SHEET 1 GREENLEAZE TO REDCATCH RD 1940s.

COWBOY LANE

UNLET UNIT

BROTHER TO DICKY AT WELLS RD SCHOOL A TEACHER

BANDAGES AND BLOOD. "WILL YOU STOP BLOWING IN MY FACE SON?"

SOLD OUT AS SWEET RATION -ING STOPPED TEMPORARILY IN 1949.

4 GALLONS PLEASE HAVE YOU GOT CHANGE OF A POUND?

RED LION GARAGE.

BANISTER AND DAYS

BUSSEY/ DIMOND.

PAPER STAND FOR MR EAST ERBROOK AND HIS SUCCESORS

MISS BANISTER RETIRED, THEN LIVED AT 38 AIRPORT RD.

HERE'S THE BUS COMING. "GIT YER POST, READ ALL ABHAT IT". "ABOUT WHAT MY BOY?? OH WHATEVERS INIT SIR".

L A England 2012

SHEET 1 OTHER SIDE OF WELLS RD.   GREENMORE RD TO RED LION HILL 1940s TALBOT LANE

HURFORDS BUILDERS- YARD AND A BARBER

BARBERS

CRIS GAY

W.A. WAKEFIELD

JACKSONS STORES

CO-OPERATIVE

TO SCHOOL →
TO HOME →
MONDAY NIGHTS
FETCH GROCERIES

MANAGER MR SAUNDERS.	MNGR MR ALLEN	CONFECTIONER	GREENGROCER
BY COUNTER MRS NORMAN	WINE & SPIRIT MGNTS	SWEETS, TOBACCO	FLORIST.
CASHIER JOAN DERRICK	PROVISIONS		

L.A. England 2007
BUTCHER

THIS BANK
WAS HELD
UP DURING
THE SUMMER
OF 1949.

THE MANAGER WAS
SHOT AND KILLED.
NOBODY HAS EVER YET
BEEN ARRESTED AND
CHARGED WITH THE
CRIME.

G A England 2007

Circa 1869.

Mullers Homes Nuk.

From A Photo.

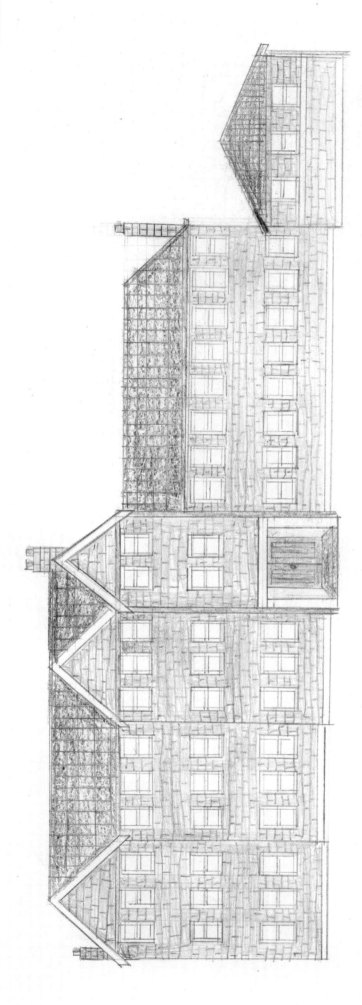

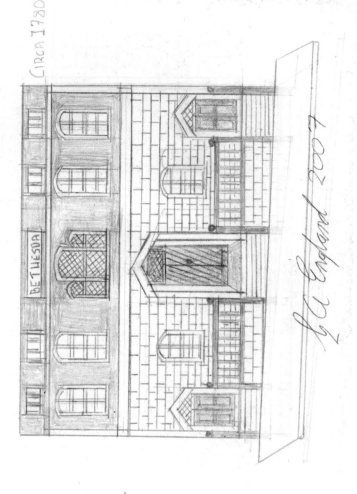

Circa 1780

BETHESDA

G. C. England 2007

George Mullers Place Of Worship
In Great George St. Another Sad
Victim Of The Blitz. ———>
On Nov 24th 1940. From A Photo.

My Maternal Grandfathers Home
From 29th Nov 1876 Until 11th Nov 1886,
As He Was Now 14 Years Of Age. He Was
Then Apprenticed To Mr William Ash A
Bootmaker Of Kingsley House Cotham
Bristol.

Bristol Landmarks

TEMPLE MEADS RAIL STN.   CIRCA 1878

THE DOME WAS A CASUALTY
OF THE BLITZ OF
25TH NOV 1940, AND
NOT REPLACED.

WITHOUT THE FRILLS AND
EMBELISHMENTS.

BRISTOL PARKWAY RAIL STATION.   IN 1982

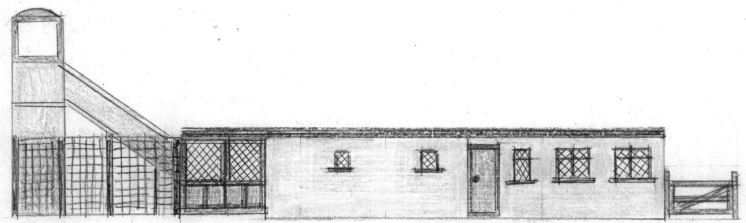

FOOTBRIDGE TO
PLATFORMS
ONE AND TWO.
PADLOCKED GATE
TO CROSSING.
WIRED FENCE.

G A England 2013

THESE SOUGHT AFTER HOUSES BACK ON TO TENNIS RD AND HAVE A VERY
COMMANDING VIEW OF THE CITY FROM UPSTAIRS.
BURNETT 67. SLOCOMBE 69.   LEE'S 71.   DELAHAYE 73.

SUSPENSION BRIDGE   CHRIST   CHESTERFIELD   ST ANDREWS   CABOT   UNIVERSITY
                     CHURCH   NURSING HOME   PARISH   TOWER   TOWER
                                                   CHURCH.

NB. SAINT ANDREWS WAS DESTROYED BY ENEMY ACTION ON 25TH NOV 1940. HOWEVER
THE TOWER SURVIVED UNTIL 1954. (CHRIST CHURCH IS NOW CLIFTONS PARISH
CHURCH). IT WAS ERECTED IN 1822 TO REPLACE AN ERLIER ONE ERECTED
IN 1654. THIS IN TURN HAD REPLACED AN EVEN EARLIER ONE FROM
THE 10TH OR 11TH CENTURY. HERE WERE LAID TO REST LT COL
BRERETON WITH HIS WIFE LYDIA, THE SHARPLES FAMILY, AND
MANY OTHERS.

G A England 2007

KING EDWARD VII   CIRCA 1912.

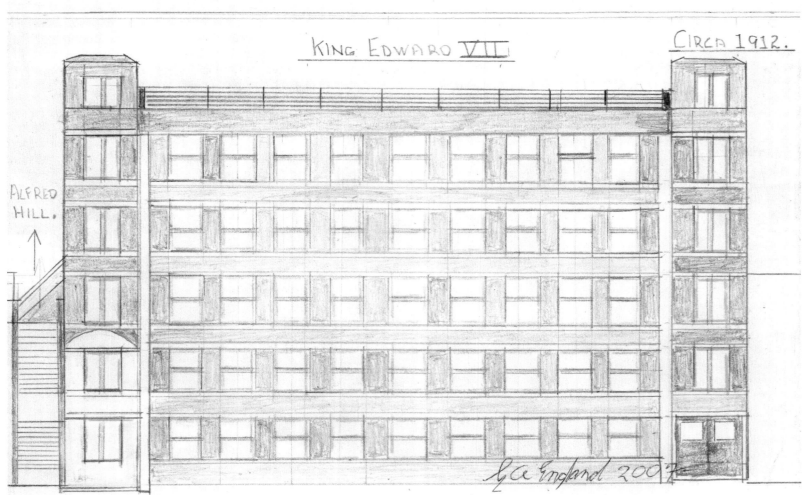

ALFRED
HILL.

Gee England 2007

BUILT BY WILLIAM PATEY
FOR JOHN PINNEY A
BRISTOL MERCHANT
AND COPIED FROM A
PHOTO. SITUATED IN Gt
GEORGE St. JOHN WAS
FATHER TO CHARLES
CHAS BEING THE MAYOR
OF BRISTOL AT THE
TIME OF THE RIOTS ON
SUNDAY 30th OCT 1831.

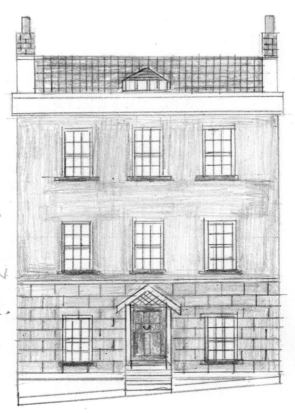

CAMP HOUSE.   CIRCA 1831.

BUILT BY CHARLES DYER
FOR CHARLES PINNEY.
HE WAS JOHNS SON.
ALSO MAYOR OF BRISTOL
AT THE TIME OF THE
RIOTS OF 1831. AT
ONE TIME POST WAR
THE RESIDENCE OF DR
RAMSAY GARDEN. IT
IS NOW ENGINEERS HSE
AND THE PROPERTY OF
THE AEU. DONE
PURELY FROM MEMORY.
SITUATED IN THE
PROMENADE CLIFTON DOWN.
FORMER ROMAN ENCAMPMENT NEARBY. ⟶

G A England 2007
TO SUSPENSION BRIDGE ⟶

PATH TO BEACH.

1947. REDCLIFFE BAY PORTISHEAD AT LOW TIDE. LOOKING OVER TO SOUTH WALES.

Bill England 2009
AUNTY JEANS
THE ALWYNS.

MR WORREL THE BUTCHERS.

FISHING SLOOP GONE AGROUND 1938. THREE LIVES LOST.

FISHING SLOOP GONE AGROUND 1947.

FAMILY HOLIDAY 1947.

BYcc.

FROM A PHOTO(S)   3 PRISONS   BRISTOL NEW GAOL   CIRCA 1820.

SITUATED IN CUMBERLAND RD THIS PRISON WAS REPLACED BY HORFIELD IN 1883. UNTIL 1849 PUBLIC HANGINGS TOOK PLACE ON A PLATFORM ATOP THE MAIN GATE. THIS GATE AND ITS SURROUND IS ALL THAT IS LEFT NOW. THE LAST EXECUTION TOOK PLACE IN GREAT BRITAIN IN 1964.

BRIDEWELL ST POLICE STATION AND GAOL. FOR PRISONERS ON REMAND.

HORFIELD GAOL CIRCA 1883. SITUATED IN CAMBRIDGE RD.

G a England 2011.

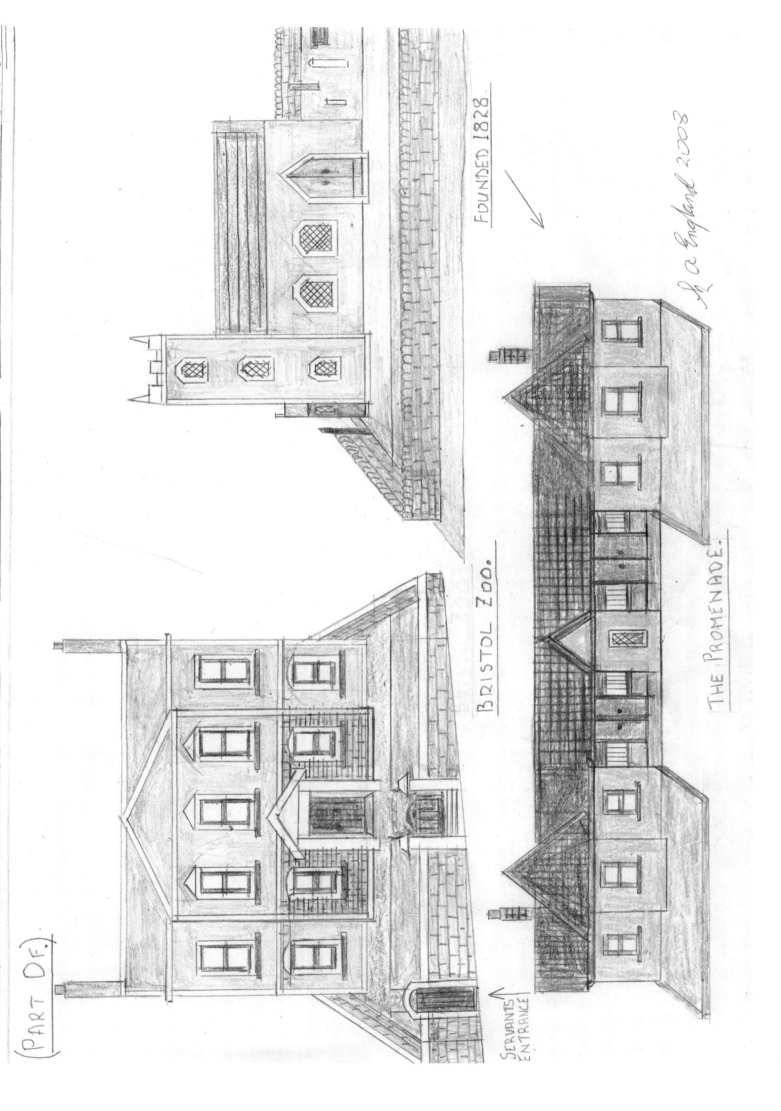

Chesterfield House, Circa 1750. · Clifton Hill, Clifton Parish Church, Circa 1654.

(Part Of.)

Servants Entrance

Bristol Zoo.

Founded 1828

The Promenade.

J. A. England 2008

Notes on *Future Perfect*

Garth England's drawings were discovered during the research phase of a public art programme in Hengrove, south Bristol, called *Future Perfect*.

Co-curated by Jes Fernie and Theresa Bergne *Future Perfect* was developed following a wide-ranging series of workshops, artist talks, and excursions with local residents, to explore the potential of public art in the area. Many people felt that young people should be at the centre of the programme. With this in mind, the curators devised a theme that focused on the concept of the future; a notional, fantastical future which embraces extraordinary possibilities and dreams.

The first *Future Perfect* commission, *Archive of Ideas* by Martino Gamper, was a flexible, peripatetic display structure that provided a catalyst for conversations about the art programme, people's ambitions for Hengrove, and their views on the area as a whole. The archive, made up of artists' proposals, photographs of the area, books and people's responses to the programme, was set up and displayed in a large number of public places in Hengrove, including the leisure centre, churches and the local library and community hall.

Nils Norman was commissioned to make a work that helped knit together the disparate green spaces in the neighbourhood. *Pieces of Play*, Norman's collective title for his project, consists of a generous public footpath, a series of discreet play areas that encourage imaginative interaction amongst children, and a new theatre curtain for Hengrove Community Centre that references the history of the neighbourhood. The collage of images on the curtain includes a number of drawings by Garth England that also appear in this book.

The third and final *Future Perfect* commission is David Thorpe's orchard on Whitchurch Village Green which was planted in the winter of 2015. The design of the orchard mimics the floor plan of a cathedral and creates a 'great hall' within which the community can congregate, celebrate the passing of the seasons, hold picnics and social events, and learn horticultural skills.

A proposal by Matt Stokes to make a science fiction film that imagined a future Hengrove, in collaboration with young people in the area, remains unrealised. However, Stokes' research material and notes for *The Venturers* can be seen on the *Future Perfect* website, along with further information and interviews with the other three artists.

Future Perfect is part of a wider programme of public art commissions in Bristol, one of the UK's leading cities for public art commissioning. It was funded by developers who delivered a number of public amenities on the west side of Hengrove Park. The funds were devolved by Bristol City Council planners to a local group known as a Neighbourhood Partnership in an effort to ensure that the programme reflected the needs and wishes of local people.

Murdered by Straight Lines: drawings of Bristol by Garth England has come out of the *Future Perfect* programme through a process of serendipity and good fortune. As with all genuinely embedded public art projects, this book and the commissions outlined above, are the result of conversations with local people that build on pre-existing stories and dreams.

www.futureperfectbristol.org
www.aprb.co.uk

Thank you to
Mike Leigh, Knowle and Totterdown
Local History Society
Geoff Gardiner, Whitchurch Local History Society
Staff at Hengrove Lodge, Residential Care Home
Jane Gould, Whitchurch Library

Future Perfect Advisory Group:
Ray Andrews
John Button
Norma Davies
Trevor Davies
Bob Fisher
Ron Gilliard
Paula Painter, Oasis Academy John Williams
Bill Roberts
Charlotte Smith, Youth Moves
Nella Stokes, South Bristol Skills Academy
Jean Young, Hengrove Community Centre

Local Councillors from Hengrove Ward:
Barry Clark
Sylvia Doubell
Michael Frost

Bristol City Council:
Ariaf Hussain, Neighbourhood Partnership Coordinator
Aldo Rinaldi, Senior Public Art Officer

Jes Fernie and Theresa Bergne
would like to thank:
Ray Andrews
Alex Barry
John Button
Helen Davies
Martino Gamper
Andy Gibbins
Jason Glynos
Nils Norman
Matt Stokes
David Thorpe

Future Perfect team:
Aldo Rinaldi, Commissioner
Jes Fernie and Theresa Bergne, Co-curators
Jo Plimmer, Engagement Curator
Leela Clarke, Marketing Manager
Lynn Froggett, Evaluator
Tessa Fitzjohn, Project Manager (Community Orchard)

Editors
Jes Fernie
Theresa Bergne

Assistant Editor
Hannah Wainwright

Design by
Stefan Kraus and Lisa Stephanides
Polimekanos

Printed and bound by
Graphius, Ghent

Drawings scanned by
Niche Frames, Bristol

First published in 2016 by
Redcliffe Press Ltd
81g Pembroke Road
Clifton
Bristol BS8 3EA
www.redcliffepress.co.uk

Every care has been taken to trace residents
identified in this publication. We apologise for any
infringement where this information has proved
untraceable.

ISBN 978-1-908326-94-2

Images © copyright
Mike Leigh, Knowle and
Totterdown Local History Society

Texts © copyright the authors

Garth England's drawings are available to view
at Bristol Record Office.

British Library Cataloguing-in-Publication Data
A catalogue record for this book is available
from the British Library.